THE 1999 COMPLETE

FOR MICHIGAN

Listing Every Known Antique Shop and Mall in the State

Plus for Many Shops:

Days & Hours of Operation
Directions for Finding Shop & Malls
Detailed Maps Showing Locations
Size or Specialty of the Shop

Published by:
Complete Antique Shop Directories
P.O. Box 297
Lakeside MI 49116
616-469-2433; Fax 616-469-0455
E-mail: AntiqueDir@aol.com

Edward Lawrence, Publisher
Michelle Budak, Administrative Assistant

THE 1999 COMPLETE ANTIQUE SHOP DIRECTORY FOR MICHIGAN

- - *Table of Contents* - -

Map of Michigan, Lower Peninsula

3 > Tier number   3.4 > County Sequence Number

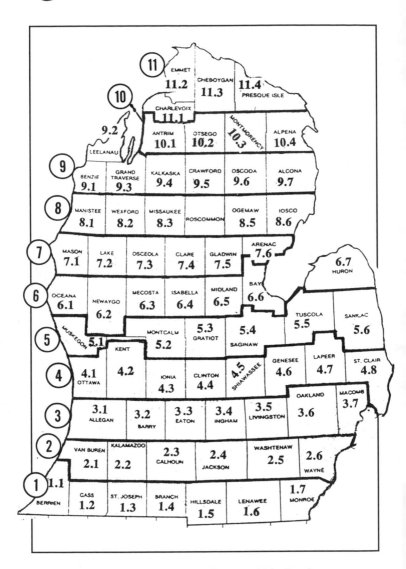

Tier 1   Along the Indiana & Ohio Border
Tier 2   Kalamazoo-Homer-Detroit
Tier 3   Saugatuck-Lansing-Royal Oak
Tier 4   Grand Rapids-Flint-Port Huron
Tier 5   The M-46 Route
Tier 6   The M-20 Route
Tier 7   Ludington-Gladwin-Standish
Tier 8   The M-55 Route
Tier 9   The M-72 Route
Tier 10   The M-32 Route
Tier 11   South of Mackinac

Map of Michigan, Upper Peninsula

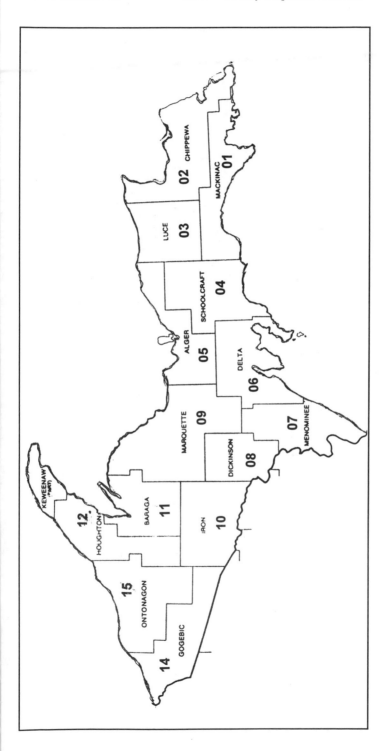

INDEX OF TOWNS AND CITIES

City, *County Sequence Number, County* , Page

Index of Cities and Towns - continued

Index of Cities and Towns - continued

Index of Cities and Towns - continued

INDEX OF COUNTIES

Tier & County Sequence Number to left, Page Number to right.

INTRODUCTION

This Antique Shop Directory lists all the antique shops and malls that could be identified in the state of Michigan. Every establishment was invited to help support the cost of preparing and printing this book by placing a Complete Listing or a Display Ad in the book. Those shops and malls that did offer such support are listed in bold type, and their hours of operation, directions, and often a statement concerning the size or nature of the shop, are given. Those shops without such information were unwilling to contribute $45.00 toward the cost of printing this book and establishing the web site.

The publisher of this book thanks those shops who helped make publication of this book possible. In some cases additional information was given about malls or shops as a service to the user of this book, even if the shop owner was unwilling to support the cost of printing the book.

In order to make this book as user-friendly as possible for antiquers driving the area, shops are listed geographically, starting with the tier of counties at the south portion of the state and working north. Within each tier, counties are listed from west to east. The First Chapter contains those counties in the southern tier, along the Indiana and Ohio border. The Second Chapter includes the counties in the next tier of counties to the north, etc.

Within each county shops are grouped by town or city, generally moving from north to south and west to east. Maps for each county, and many cities, show locations of antique shops contributing to the cost of printing the book. **Each county has an identification number. The number to the left of the decimal point is the Tier Number. The number to the right of the decimal point is the County Sequence Number within that Tier.**

Where several antique shops are located in proximity to one another, a symbol for all may be shown on the map rather than the identification number of each. Several shops are located in Marshall, for example; Marshall is marked with an "M" on the county map.

Efforts have been made to make this Directory as complete and accurate as possible. Antique shops do close and move, however, and new ones open. The Publisher cannot be responsible for erroneous or outdated information. Users of this Directory should be aware that hours indicated are "targets", and that sometimes antique dealers go to auctions or are gone on personal business, and may not be in at a time they are normally open. Also, some dealers do shows on certain weekends. It is always best to call if you intend to drive out of your way to visit a shop.

Please send, fax, or E-mail a note to the publisher with any additions or corrections to be incorporated into the next edition.

ANTIQUES ON THE INTERNET

This year an effort has been made to obtain an E-mail address and web site address for those antique shops and malls that have them. The web sites fall into two categories: 1. Individual domain home page for the shop or mall, and: 2 A page on a larger internet site hosting listings for multiple businesses. Among some examples of the former are the following:

www.dunesantiques.com   www.lesprit.com
www.woodenskete.com   www.millingtonantiques.com

Among the examples of larger internet web sites hosting a listing for antique shops and malls are the following:

www.classic-link.com   www.theantiqueexchange.com
www.tias.com   www.antiquesring.net

These web sites have information about the shop or mall, and usually have individual antiques for sale listed and often shown.   Prospective buyers can contact the shop or mall by telephone, fax, or E-mail to obtain additional information or to arrange purchase and delivery of the item. See also: www.collectoronline.com

Another way in which the Internet is becoming of major importance to antique dealers and collectors is through the various actions conducted on the Internet. The most famous is E-Bay (www.ebay.com), but there are many others as well.   Several dealers have reported that a major proportion of their sales are now made through on-line auctions.   Registration as a buyer or seller is an easy process, explained on the web site for the respective auctions.   Among the auction web sites are the following:

www.ebay.com   www.potteryauction.com
www.antiquealley.com   www.auctionuniverse.com

In addition to using the auction web sites for buying and selling, they can be used to research the value of an item. Sales prices are usually left on-line for a time after the auction, and sites are searchable to find the type of item you want to appraise. Collectors of specific antiques or collectibles may very likely have a web site and chat-room for their area of interest, where they can learn more about the subject and make contact with other collectors of that specialty. One example of a collector web sites is for the Imperial Glass Collectors' Society: www.imperialglass.org

The Antiques & Collectibles Dealers Association has a useful web site at www.acda.org. Several antique newspapers and magazines have web sites that provide a summary of their latest issue, classified ads, as well as links to other sites of interest to antiquers. Among these are: www.antiqueweek.com (Antique Week), and www.americanantiquities.com (American Antiquities).

Additional suggestions for using the internet to buy, sell, and research antiques will be given on our own web site starting March 1999: **www.AntiqueShops.net**   For additional tips concerning Antiques on the Internet see pages 109, 139, and 212.

TIER 1:
ALONG THE INDIANA
& OHIO BORDER

1.1 Berrien County

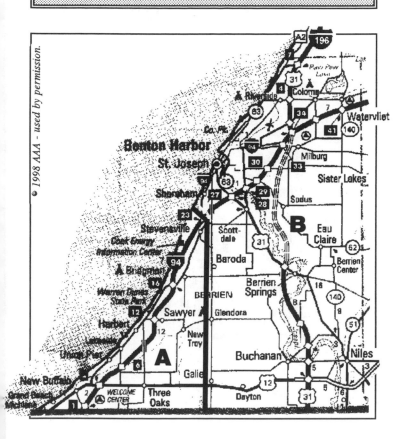

© 1998 AAA - used by permission.

Districts Within Berrien County:
      A: Southwest Berrien County: Harbor Country
      B: Eastern & Northern Berrien County

A. Southwestern Berrien County: Harbor Country

NEW BUFFALO

1   Rainbow's End Antiques
18712 LaPorte Road (Whittaker Street)
New Buffalo   MI 49117;
616 469-2655

Map of Southwest Berrien County:

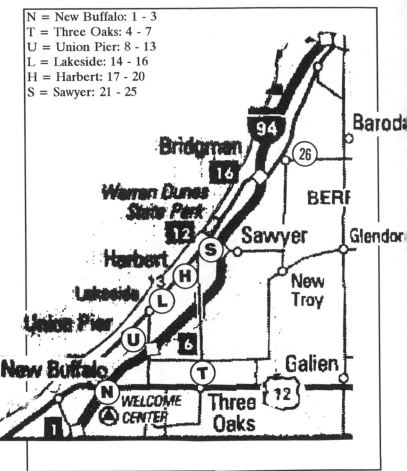

N = New Buffalo: 1 - 3
T = Three Oaks: 4 - 7
U = Union Pier: 8 - 13
L = Lakeside: 14 - 16
H = Harbert: 17 - 20
S = Sawyer: 21 - 25

© *1998 AAA - used by permission.*

2   Classic Galleries
430 South Whittaker Street
New Buffalo   MI 49117
616 469-6281; Fax: 616 469-6280
Daily 11 to 6
Midway between I-94 Exit 1 and downtown New Buffalo, west side of street.
European antiques, garden statuary, bronzes, marble, lighting, home furnishings.
Auctions several times a year.
(See full-page ad on opposite page.)

3   Antiques Inc.
U.S. Highway 12
New Buffalo   MI 49117
616 943-4456

THREE OAKS

4   Hank's Ole School House
8075 U.S. Highway 12 West
Three Oaks MI 49129
616 469-4015
Memorial Day to Labor Day: Sat. 10 to 5, Sun. 10 to 4;
Labor Day to Nov.: Weekends by chance.
Half way between New Buffalo and Three Oaks, north side of
highway, at Basswood Road.
Collectibles, antiques, resale.

5   Springdale
17 South Elm Street
Three Oaks MI 49129
616 621-3642
Summer: Every Day 11 to 6; Winter: Fri. to Mon. 11 to 6
Downtown, east side of the street, a block north of U.S. 12, in
former bowling alley.
Thirties to Fifties furniture and accessories, specializing in
Heywood Wakefield Modern.
Springdale is currently located at Lakeside Antiques, in
Lakeside.   The shop will be relocating to this location in June
1999.

"Furnishings for the Modern Family"

Jim Toler

17 S. Elm Street
Three Oaks MI
49129

Phone:
616 621-3642

6   Jenney's Antiques
9 North Elm Street
Three Oaks   MI 49128
616 756-7219;   Closed Christmas until March.

7 The Heartworks Antiques & Collectibles

1 East Central Drive
Three Oaks MI 49128
616 756-9800   616 756-7303
Memorial Day to end of Sept.: Thurs. to Mon. 11 to 5:30;
Winter: Fri. to Sun. 11 to 5:30
Half block east of downtown, just north of the tracks.
"Antiques & collectibles to warm the heart."

UNION PIER

8   The Plum Tree
16337 Red Arrow Highway
Union Pier   MI 49129
616 469-5980

9 Eagle Antique Mall

16112 Red Arrow Highway
Union Pier MI 49122
616 927-3457
Sat. & Sun. 12 to 6
West side of highway, just south of the blinker light at Union
Pier Road.
Located in a former bowling alley.
Wide variety of antiques and collectibles.

10   K.L.M. Galleries
16142 Red Arrow Highway
Union Pier MI 49129
616 469-6957

11 Twelve Cedars Vintage Furniture

16117 Red Arrow Highway
Union Pier   MI 49129
616 469-0304
Thurs. to Mon. 10 to 5
East side of the highway, just south of the blinking light at
Union Pier Road.
Old & new pine & cherry furniture; art, antiques, interior
design.

12 Frog Forest Findings

16100 York Road
Union Pier   MI 49129
616 469-7050
Fri. to Mon. 12 to 6; hours subject to change. Closed Jan.
West of I-94 Exit 6, south side of Union Pier Road.
Gas Station memorabilia, furniture, electric trains, antique
cars, and new stuff.

Map: Lakeside & Union Pier:

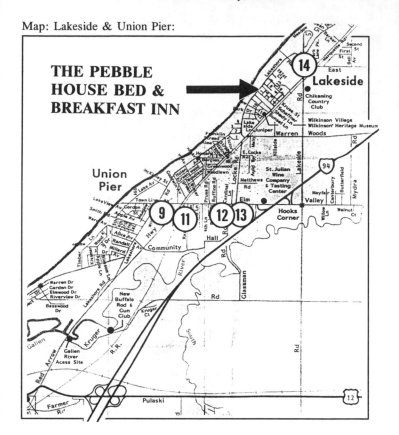

13   Antique Mall & Village
9300 Union Pier Road
Union Pier   MI 49129
616 469-2555
Mon. to Sat. 10 to 6, Sun. 12 to 6
Jan. to March: closed Tues. & Wed.
I-94 Exit 6, southwest corner.
44 dealer booths; diner open in the summer. See the recreation of the Sistine Chapel.

LAKESIDE

14   Lakeside Depot
14906 Red Arrow Highway
Lakeside MI 49116
616 469-9700   Antique & contemporary art & decorative items.

15   Lakeside Antique Center
14876 Red Arrow Highway
Lakeside   MI 49116
616 469-7717

THE PEBBLE HOUSE
BED & BREAKFAST INN

15093 Lakeshore Road
Lakeside MI 49116
616 469-1416
In the Arts & Crafts style.
Visit Our Web Site:
www.bbonline.com/mi/pebblehouse

Map: Harbert & Sawyer:

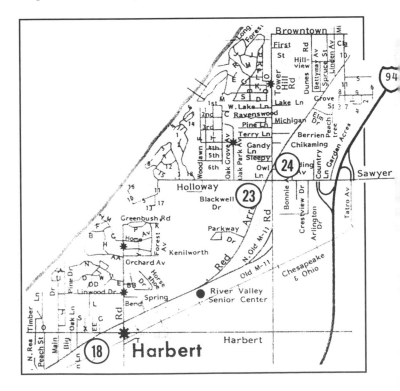

16   Lakeside Antiques
14866 Red Arrow Highway
Lakeside   MI 49116
616 469-4467
Furniture; primitives; lamps; rugs; reproductions; folk art; etc.

HARBERT

17   Kalamazoo Antiques
13701 Red Arrow Highway
Harbert   MI 49115
616 469-3511   Art pottery, 50's modern, paintings, prints, etc.

18   Harbert Antique Mall
13889 Red Arrow Highway
Harbert MI 49115
616 469-0977
Mon. to Fri. 10 to 6, Sat. 10 to 7, Sun. 12 to 7
Closed Wed. in winter.
East side of highway.
Featuring upholstered furniture, art, vintage chandeliers &
lighting, fine glass, pottery, collectibles. 50 dealers.

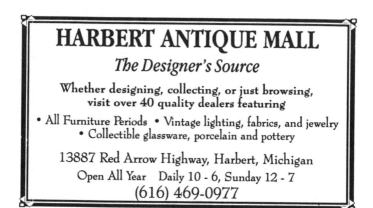

19   Marco Polo Antiques
13630 Red Arrow Highway
Harbert   MI 49115
616 469-6272

20   Callas
13446 Red Arrow Highway
Harbert MI 49115   616 469-3674

SAWYER

21   Nestings
13025 Red Arrow Highway
Sawyer MI 49125
616 426-8109   Antiques, art, home accessories.

22   Jeff's Trading Post
13212 Red Arrow Highway
Sawyer   MI 49125
616 426-3145   Hoosier Cabinets, glass, bottles, etc.

23   Timeless Treasures Antiques & Collectibles
12908 Red Arrow Highway
Sawyer   MI 49127
616 426-3636
April to Nov.: Daily 10:30 to 5:30;
Dec. to March: Thurs. to Mon. 10:30 to 5:30
Southwest corner Red Arrow Highway & Sawyer Road.
General line of antiques & collectibles.

24   Dunes Antique Center, Inc.
12825 Red Arrow Highway
Sawyer   MI 49125
Phone: 616 426-4043; Fax: 616 426-8238;
Web site: www.dunesantiques.com
E-mail: MPIPELINE@AOL.COM
Mon. to Sat. 10 to 6, Sun. 11 to 6, closed Tues.
I-94 Exit 12, then 300 yards west; east side of Red Arrow
Highway, just north of Sawyer Road.
Over 70 dealers; art, pottery, furniture, glass, etc.

25   Tara Hill Antique Mall
12816 Red Arrow Highway, north of Sawyer Road
Sawyer   MI 49125
616 426-8673
Ask about antique restoration services available.

BRIDGMAN

26   Rideout Antiques
4369 Lake Street
Bridgman   MI 49106
616 465-6855
Mon. to Fri. 10 to 5; Sun. 1 to 6;
Closed Centerville Sundays and April 1 to 18.
Red Arrow Highway to stoplight, east on Lake St. (Shawnee Road); tan & tiel stucco 2 story building on left.
Glass, china, silverplate, vintage, & unusual small items.

STEVENSVILLE

27   Bill's Real Antiques
7566 Red Arrow Highway
Stevensville   MI 49127
616 465-3246

B. Eastern & Northern Berrien County

NILES

Note: One shop with a Niles address is located in Cass County.

28   Picker's Paradise Antique Mall
2809 South 11th Street (Highway M-51)
Niles   MI 49120
616 683-6644
Every day, 10 to 6
East side of highway, between Niles and South Bend.
107 dealers, 30,000 square feet.

29   Antiques & More
2429 South 11th Street
Niles   MI 49120
616 683-4222

30   Michiana Antique Mall
2423 South 11th Street
Niles   MI 49120
616 684-7001; 800 559-4694
E-mail: michianaantiquemall@compuserve.com
Web-site: www.michianaantiquemall.com
7 days, 10 to 6 (Closed four major holidays.)
East side of highway, between Niles and South Bend.
94 dealers, 27,000 square feet; air conditioned.

Map: Eastern & Northern Berrien County:

N = **Niles Downtown:** 31 - 39

B = **Baroda:** 39 - 41

W = **Watervliet:**
    47 - 50

196

53

31

4

Coloma

51

63

34

7

Watervliet

41

140

94

Benton Harbor

Milburg

30

46

Sister Lakes

45

St. Joseph

6

44

29

9

2

42

Sodus

4

43

Scott-
dale

31

Eau
Claire

62

Baroda

Berrien
Center

B

Berrien
Springs

140

Glendora

51

Buchanan

Niles

N

12

28

Dayton

31

30

© *1998 AAA - used by permission.*

23

31   Oak Street Antiques & Collectibles
1008 Oak Street
Niles MI 49120

32   Yankee Heirloom
211 North 2nd Street
Niles MI 49120   616 684-0462

33   Four Flags Antique Mall
218 North 2nd Street
Niles   MI 49120
616 683-6681
Summer: Mon. to Sat. 10 to 6, Sun. 12 to 6;
Winter: Mon. to Fri. 10 to 5, Sat. 10 to 6, Sun. 12 to 6
Downtown, half block north of the main street.
22,000 square feet, 60 dealers.

34   Niles Antique Mall
220 North Front Street
Niles MI 49120   616 683-6652

35   Antique Haven
207 North Second Street
Niles MI 49120
(616) 683-8150; or 616 445-5150
E-Mail: aynetiqu@aol.com
Tues. to Sat. 10 to 7, Sun. 12 to 6
Just north of the main street, across from Four Flags Antique
Mall.
Fine country antiques and smalls.
Antique and household appraisals by Jayme-Ayne Rich.

36   This & That Marketplace
2622 South 11th Street
Niles MI 49120
616 683-6149

BUCHANAN

37   Millrace Antiques & Collectibles
122 East Front Street
Buchanan   MI 49107
616 695-2005

BERRIEN SPRINGS

38   More & More Antiques & Collectibles
6659 U.S. 31 & 33, south of Rocky Weed Road
Berrien Springs   MI 49103
616 428-9084

BARODA

39   Shawnee Road Antiques
638 East Shawnee Road
Baroda   MI 49101
616 422-1382
April to Dec. 1: Every day 1 to 5;
Winter: Sat. & Sun. by chance or appointment.
Between Berrien Springs and Bridgman, south side of road.
Furniture, quality smalls and collectibles.

40   Homeless Treasures
9012 First Street
Baroda MI 49101
616 422-6110;   Fax: 616-422-6129;   E-Mail: homtr@aol.com
Every day 10:30 to 6
Two blocks south of intersection of Stevensville-Baroda Road
and Lemon Creek Road.
Wide assortment of antiques and furniture.   Also custom
furniture refinishing and repair; all furniture is hand stripped.

41   Classics
9004 First Street
Baroda   MI 49101
616 422-1991
Mon. to Sat. 10 to 5:30; closed Jan. to April 1.
Downtown
Floral shop, gifts, and antiques.   Also: furniture refinishing and
mirror resilvering.

SODUS

42   Virgo Antiques
4106 River Road
Sodus   MI 49126
616 927-3880
Sat. & Sun. 12 to 5; other days by chance; closed Jan. 1 to
May 1
From Exit 29 of I-94 go south on Pipestone Road, left at stop
sign, right on River Road.
Primitives, cut glass, etc.

ST. JOSEPH

43   Anvil Antiques
3439 Hollywood Road
St. Joseph   MI 49085
616 429-5132
East from I-94 Exit 27 on M-63 1 block, south on Hollywood
one block.

Map: St. Joseph & Benton Harbor:

44   Miller's Antiques & Collectibles
719 Gard Avenue
St. Joseph MI 49085
616 983-2900; Fax: 616 983-2940
Mon. to Fri. 10 to 5, Sat. 10 to 3
From I-94 go north on Niles Avenue (M-63) past Hilltop
Street; between Wendy's and Subway go west on Gard 1/2
block; north side of street.

45   Days of Yore
215 State Street
St. Joseph   MI 49085
616 983-4144
E-mail: cbyore@cpuinc.net
Mon. to Sat. 10 to 5, Sun. 12 to 5
Downtown, east side of the street. One block west of
Business 94
Furniture, 50's items, jewelry, china, glass, misc.

*NOTE: The second floor of Silver Beach Emporium at 217
State next door has a branch of More & More Antiques of
Berrien Springs with some antiques and used books.*

■ BENTON HARBOR ■

46   Good Old Times Antiques
3076 East Napier Avenue
Benton Harbor   MI 49022
616 925-8422
Most days: 1 to 4 by chance or appointment.
1 mile east of I-94 Exit 30, south side of road.
Large selection of quality furniture and accessories.

WATERVLIET

47   All Military Antiques
324 North Main Street
Watervliet MI 49098
616 463-4917
Mon. to Sat. 10 to 5, Sun. 12 to 5
Downtown, east side of the street, next to the bank.
Military items from the Civil War to the present, specializing
in World Wars I and II.

48   Trade Winds Antiques
336 North Main Street
Watervliet   MI 49098
616 463-8281
Every Day 10 to 5; Sun. 12 to 5
I-94 Exit 41, north to Downtown; east side of the street.
Collectibles, glass, postcards, and a general line.   Also: full
service bead store.

49   Old World Antiques
349 North Main Street
Watervliet   MI 49098
616 463-2888
Tues. to Fri. 10 to 6; Sat. 10 to 5; Sun. 12 to 5
Center of town, west side of the main street. Exit 41 off I-94,
exit 18 off I-196.
Victorian, primitives, Civil War, 19th Century military, vintage
collectibles.
28 dealers, 6,000 square feet.
House of David Museum on site.
*(See information about the House of David on the following
page.)*

50   Z's Antiques
7579 Red Arrow Highway West
Watervliet   MI 49098
616 463-5487

COLOMA

51   Linda's Antiques & Crafts
120 North Church Street
Coloma MI 49038
616 468-7917
Daily 10 to 6, closed Thurs.
From I-94, go to 3rd stop light, left next to park in little white
house.
Collectibles, glassware, crafts, paintings, jewelry, etc.

52   The Millstone Shop
6162 Martin Road
Coloma   MI 49038
616 468-6667
East from I-96 (Exit 7) on Hagar Shore then south on Martin.

53   Myrt's Antiques & Collectibles
82331 45th Avenue
Coloma MI 49038
616 849-0536
Summer: Every day 8 to 7, but call first;
Winter: Every day 10 to 4
From I-196 take Exit 7 west to the Blue Star Highway, then
go north 2.5 miles to 145th Street and go right; shop is in the
rear of the first house to the right.
Furniture, glassware, collectibles, etc.

THE HOUSE OF DAVID

**The House of David is a religious colony founded in
1903 by Benjamin and Mary Purcell in Benton Harbor,
Michigan.   The colony grew to over one thousand members in the 1930's. There was a world-champion base-
ball team, orchestras and bands, a 500 acre amusement
park with 8 miniature trains, a zoo with animals from
throughout the world, and the largest tourist court in
America at the time.   The members produced beautiful
art and furniture.   Some of the buildings still remain in
Benton Harbor, and the House of David Museum at the
Old World Antiques shop in Watervliet is assembling
mementos of the House of David.**

1.2 Cass County

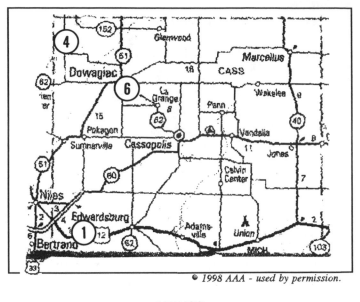

© 1998 AAA - used by permission.

NILES

Note: The main part of Niles is in Berrien County, Section 1.1.

1 B. & J. Antiques
3185 Follmer Street
Niles MI 49120 -- 2.5 miles west of Edwardsburg
616 663-8354
Tues. to Sat. 12 to 5:30, Sun. by Chance.
8 miles east of Niles, 2.5 miles west of Edwardsburg, north of
U.S. 12 between Anderson & Bebee Streets.
General line.

EDWARDSBURG

2   Argus Antiques
26878 West Main Street (U.S. 12)
Edwardsburg   MI 49112
616 663-2883

EAU CLAIRE

3   Oak Hill Antiques
6520 Brush Lake Road, at Eureka Road
Eau Claire   MI 49098
616 782-9292

4   Walmar Antiques
55007 Brush Lake Road
Eau Claire   MI 49111
616 782-2315
Open by appointment or chance. It's the Huff residence, so
they are there most of the time.
Corner of Brush Lake & Eureka Roads, a quarter mile north
of Indian Lake Golf Course.
Furniture, glass, pottery, & primitives.

DOWAGIAC

5   Olympia Books and Prints
208 South Front Street
Dowagiac   MI 49047
616 782-3443
www.abebooks.com/home/olympia
Open by appointment only.

6   The Golden Acorn
202 South Front Street
Dowagiac MI 49047
616 782-1160; Fax: 616 782-1062
Gifts, antiques, and home accessories.

1.3 St. Joseph County

© 1998 AAA - used by permission.

CONSTANTINE

1   J & K Floral & Country Cupboard
145 South Washington
Constantine   MI 49042
616 435-2175
Flowers, gifts, and some antiques.

2   Antique Stoppe
63941 U.S. 131 North
Constantine   MI 49042
616 435-9445
Two miles north of Constantine, east side of highway.

THREE RIVERS

3   Nettie Dee's Antiques
25 North Main Street
Three Rivers MI 49093
616 273-9579
Tues. to Sat. 10:30 to 5:30; Sun. & Mon. by chance.
Downtown
Dolls, Carnival Glass, furniture, quality dishes, etc.

4   Antoinettes Antiques
51 North Main Street
Three Rivers   MI 49093
616 273-3333

5   Olde Town Antiques
58 North Main Street
Three Rivers   MI 49093
616 273-2596
Daily 10 to 5, Sun. 12 to 5, closed Tues.
Downtown, west side of street.
Furniture and a general line of antiques.

6   Links to the Past
52631 U.S. 131
Three Rivers   MI 49093
616 279-7310
Mon. to Sat. 10 to 6, Sun. 11 to 5, closed Wed.
Mid-way between Three Rivers & Schoolcraft, east side of
highway U.S. 131 (20 minutes from the Indiana State line).
Antiques, books, collectibles; 3,000 square feet.

7   Polish Peddler
52700 North U.S. 131
Three Rivers   MI 49093
616 273-1412
Barn in back of the house; across the highway from Links to
the Past.

STURGIS

8   The Collectors' Place
208 East Chicago Road (U.S. 12)
Sturgis MI 49091
616 659-6066
In the Premier Properties Building.

9   Antiques
1904 East Chicago
Sturgis   MI 49091
616 651-6455
Garage on the side of the house.

10   Jan Douglas Antiques
30205 East Fawn River Road
Sturgis   MI 49091
616 651-7471
4 miles southeast of town.

COLON

11   Soupy Sales
M-86 West
Colon   MI 49040
616 432-2953
North side of the highway.

12   Village Posy Shoppe
210 East State Street
Colon   MI 49040
616 432-2429
Gifts and antiques.

LEONIDAS

13   Remember When Antique Mall
100 M-60
Leonidas MI
616 496-3595

1.4 Branch County

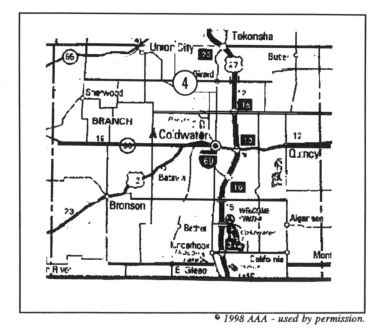

© 1998 AAA - used by permission.

BRONSON

1   Shackleton's Antiques
103 East Chicago
Bronson   MI 49028
No telephone listed.
Seldom open.

QUINCY

2   Collector's Paradise Antique Mall
47 East Chicago Road (U.S. 12)
Quincy MI 49082
No telephone listed.
Parking is in the rear.

3   Mel's Antique Emporium
929 U.S. Highway 12
Quincy MI 49082
No telephone listed.
Antiques in the rough in rear warehouse.

UNION CITY

4   Raymond's Country Barn Antiques
950 Union City Road
Union City   MI 49094
517 279-9370
Mid-way between Union City and Coldwater, north side of
road, just east of Burlington Road.

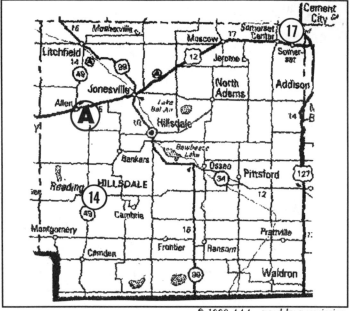

© 1998 AAA - used by permission.

A = Allen: shops 1 - 13

ALLEN

1   Brown's Antiques & Refinishing
9260 West Chicago Road
Allen MI 49227
517 869-6969
Mission oak, furniture.

2   Capital Antiques
9115 West Chicago Road
Allen   MI 49227
517 869-2055
Large mall with antiques, crafts, and reproductions.

3   Allen Antique Mall
9011 West Chicago Road (U.S. 12)
Allen   MI 49227
517 869-2788
Mon. to Sat. 10 to 5; Sun. 11 to 5
Southwest corner U.S. 12 & Duck Lake Road, west of town.
48,000 square feet; 427 dealers, representing 6 states.

4   Chicago Pike Antiques
211 West Chicago Road
Allen   MI 49227
517 869-2719
Thurs. to Mon. 10:30 to 5:30 or later.
West side of town, south side of U.S. 12.
Small group shop with fine furnishings, art & Depression
Glass, collectibles, jewelry, prints, post cards, some toys, etc.

5   Peddlers Alley
162 West Chicago Road
Allen   MI 49227
517 869-2280

6   160 W. Chicago Antiques
160 West Chicago Road
Allen   MI 49227
517 869-2929
Every day 11 to 6
Downtown, west of light, north side of the street.
Victorian furniture, glassware, Empire furniture, lamps, etc.

7   Timeless Treasures
129 West Chicago Road
Allen   MI 49227

8   Andy's Antiques
118 West Chicago Road
Allen   MI 49227
517 869-2182

9   Old Allen Township Hall Shops
114 West Chicago Road
Allen   MI 49227
517 869-2575
Every day 10 to 5
Downtown, north side of street.
Cowboy & Indian folk & tribal art; vintage clothing; Heisey
Glass.

10   Simple Pleasures
109 West Chicago Road
Allen   MI 49227
517 869-2875

11   Hand & Hearts Antiques & Folk Carvings
109 West Chicago Road
Allen   MI 49068
517 869-2553

12   Michiana Antiques
100-104 West Chicago Road
Allen   MI 49227
517 869-2132

13   A Horse of Course
108 Prentiss
Allen   MI 49227
517 869-2527
Seldom open.
Furniture in the rough & other antiques.

READING

14   The Finer Things
112 East Michigan Street
Reading   MI 49274
517 283-2451
Wed. to Fri. 10 to 5, Sat. 10 to 12, Closed Jan. 1 to May 1.
Downtown, across from post office, north side of street.

SOMERSET CENTER

15   Village Antiques
12195 U.S. Highway 12
Somerset Center MI 49282
517 688-5558

16   Bob's Antiques
12611 Chicago Road (U.S. 12)
Somerset Center   MI 49282
517 688-3596

SOMERSET

17 Oak Hill Antiques
10250 Somerset Road (U.S. 12)
Somerset MI 49281
517 547-4195
Daily: 10 to 6:30, Sun. 12 to 5, closed Tues.
One mile west of U.S. 12 & 127, north side of the highway.
Fine furniture & collectibles, lamp restoration (oil & electric),
lamp shades, furniture repair, picture frame restoration &
framing.

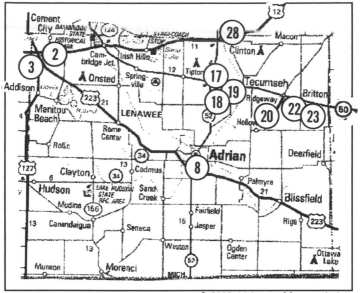

© 1998 AAA - used by permission.

HUDSON

1   Main Street Collectibles
400 West Main
Hudson MI 49247
517 448-7495

CEMENT CITY

2   Wayside Antiques
16978 U.S. Highway 12
Cement City   MI 49233
517 592-8913
Sat. & Sun. 10 to 6, Mon. to Fri. by chance or appointment.
1.5 miles east of U.S. 127, corner of U.S. 12 & Cement City
Highway.   Adjacent to the old Silver Creek Taverne &
Stagecoach Stop at the western perimeter of the Irish Hills.
A diverse collection of "trinkets and treasurers," with emphasis
on the 30's to the 60's.   "Lots of fun items -- the little things
that make your house into a collector's home."

3   Artesian Wells Antique Mall
U.S. Highways 12 & 127
Cement City   MI 49233
517 547-7422   Large good quality mall.

Map: Irish Hills Area:

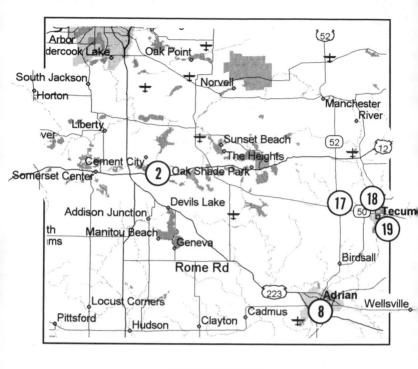

BROOKLYN

NOTE: The main part of Brooklyn, with three antique shops, is located in Jackson County.

4   The Enchanted Schoolhouse
14012 U.S. Highway 12, west of M-50
Brooklyn   MI 49230
517 592-4365

5   Muggsie's Antiques and Collectibles
13982 West U.S. Highway 12
Brooklyn MI 49230
517 592-2659

6   Brick Walker Tavern Antiques
11705 U.S. Highway 12
Brooklyn MI 49230
517 467-6961

7   Irish Hills Antiques
10600 U.S. Highway 12
Brooklyn MI 49230
517 467-4646

ADRIAN

Map: Adrian:

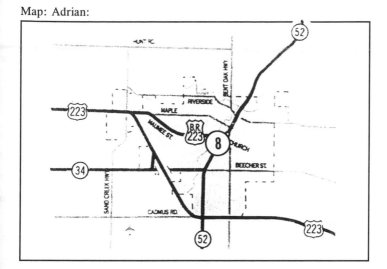

8   Marsh's Antique Mall
136 South Winter Street
Adrian MI 49221
517 263-8826
Mon. to Sat. 10 to 5:30, Sun. 1 to 5
Downtown, west side of street between Maumee & Church
Streets, one block west of Main Street.
General line of antiques.

9   Birdsall Depot
4106 North Adrian (M-52 North)
Adrian MI 49221
517 265-7107
Small shop in back of printing company.

BLISSFIELD

10   J & B Antiques Mall
109 West Adrian Street (U.S. Highway 223)
Blissfield MI 49228
517 486-3544
82 dealers

11   Blissfield Antique Mall
101 West Adrian Street
Blissfield MI 49228
517 486-2236
50 dealers

12   Williams Crossroads
10003 Adrian Street (U.S. 223 East)
Blissfield MI 49228
517 486-3315

13   Memories on Lane Street
104 South Lane Street
Blissfield   MI 49228
517 486-2327

14   Blissfield General Store: Antiques, Gifts, Sundries.
105 South Lane
Blissfield   MI 49228
517 486-5060

15   Green's Gallery Of Antiques
115 South Lane Street
Blissfield MI 49228
517 486-3080

16   Estes Antique Mall
116-118 South Lane
Blissfield MI 49228
517 486-4616

━━━━ TECUMSEH ━━━━

17 Hitching Post Antique Mall
1322 East Monroe Road
Tecumseh MI 49286
517 423-8277
Open 7 days a week: 10 to 5:30
2 mi. West of Tecumseh on M-50 near M-52
Lamp parts, hardware, books on antiques, dolls, Steiff animals.

18 Tecumseh Antique Mall
1111 West Chicago Blvd. (M-50)
Tecumseh MI 49286
517 423-6082
Mon. to Sat. 10 to 5; Sun 12 to 5
North side of M-50, west end of town.
Large good quality mall.

19   Harold Robert Antiques \ Great Ideas
154 East Chicago Blvd. (M-50)
Tecumseh MI 49286
517 423-6094
Mon. to Fri. 9 to 6:00, Sat. 9 to 5; Sun. 12 to 5
East end of downtown, south side of the street.
Fine furniture.

RIDGEWAY

20   Ridgeway Home Center
8306 East M-50
Ridgeway MI 49229
517 451-8232
E-Mail: fogelson@ini.net
Mon. to Sat. 9 to 5
North side of the highway.
Amish furniture, and antiques.

BRITTON

21   YesterYears Antiques and Estate Sales
208 East Chicago (M-50)
Britton MI 49229
517 451-8600

22   McKinney's Collectibles
108 East Chicago (M-50)
Britton MI 49229
517 451-2155
Mon. to Fri. 2 to 6; Sat. 10 to 5, or by appointment.
Eight miles west of U.S. 23, south side of the highway.
Complete line of comics and collectible cards. Beer signs,
and the world's largest beer can store.

23   Britton Village Antiques
132 Chicago Boulevard (M-50)
Britton MI 49229
517 451-8129
Thurs. to Sun. 10 to 5:30
Just west of the tracks, downtown Britton, south side of
street.

24   Yesterday's Dreams
124 East Chicago Boulevard (M-50)
Britton MI 49287
517 431-9174
E-mail: dreams@ini.net

CLINTON

25   Old Homestead Antiques
2519 West U.S. 12, west of M-52
Clinton MI 49236
517 456-4352

26   The Rose Patch
162 West Michigan
Clinton MI 49236
517 456-6473

27   Turn of the Century Lighting
116 West Michigan (U.S. 12)
Clinton MI 49236
517 456-6019
Hundreds of antique lighting fixtures in stock.

28   First Class Antique Mall
112 East Michigan Avenue
Clinton   MI 49236
517 456-6410

29   Oak City Antiques
1101 East U.S. 12
Clinton   MI 49236
517 456-4444

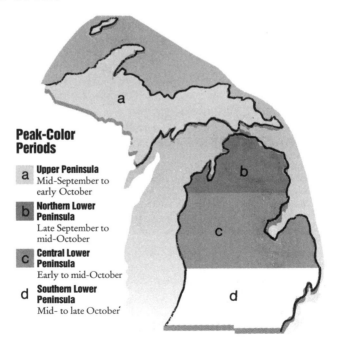

Peak-Color Periods

a **Upper Peninsula**
Mid-September to
early October

b **Northern Lower Peninsula**
Late September to
mid-October

c **Central Lower Peninsula**
Early to mid-October

d **Southern Lower Peninsula**
Mid- to late October

1.7 Monroe County

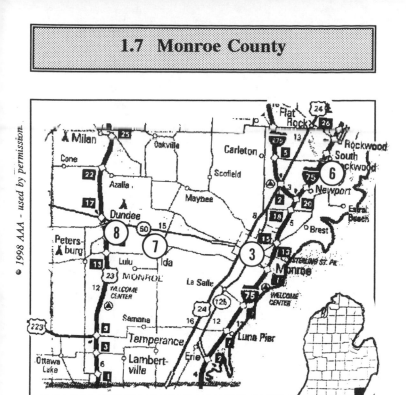

© 1998 AAA - used by permission

LaSALLE

1   American Heritage Antique Mall
5228 South Otter Creek Road, I-75 Exit 9.
LaSalle MI 48145
734 242-3430

ERIE

2   Gedert's A Touch of the Past
7442 South Dixie
Erie   MI 48133
734 848-8731

MONROE

3   Sauer Furniture & Antiques
15300 South Dixie Highway (M-125)
Monroe MI 48161-3773
734 242-6284
Tues. to Fri. 10 to 6, Sat. 10 to 5; Sundays before Christmas.
I-75 to Exit 11, west one mile to Dunbar, left one mile to
M-125, left one quarter mile.
Used furniture, antiques and collectibles.

Map: Monroe:

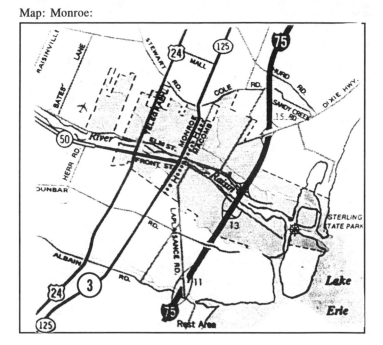

4   Spainhower's Antiques
315 South Monroe
Monroe MI 48161
734 242-5411
Mostly an auction house, but may have some items for sale
between auctions.

NEWPORT

5   The Grainery
9093 Armstrong Road
Newport MI 48166
734 586-8252
Antique and new furniture; housewares.

6   J & L Antiques and Country
8207 North Dixie Highway
Newport   MI 48166
734 586-8506
Thurs. to Sat. 10 to 5
Two miles northeast of town, west side of highway, next to
St. Charles Cemetery.   In a big 111 year old brick farm
house.
Affordable antiques; country wood crafts - custom orders
accepted.

IDA

7   Derrys of Ida
2866 Lewis Ave.
Ida MI 48140
734 269-2480
Antiques & crafts.

DUNDEE

8   Dundee Antique Shoppe
141 Riley Street
Dundee MI 48131
734 529-9007

Map: Van Buren County:

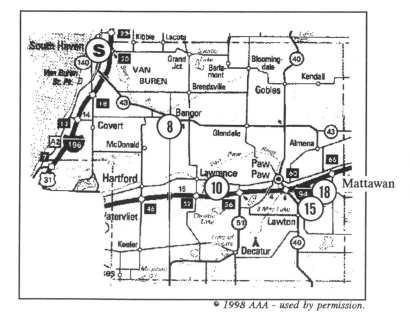

© *1998 AAA - used by permission.*

S = South Haven: 1 - 6

Van Buren County antique shop listings begin
on the following page.

TIER 2:
KALAMAZOO-HOMER-DETROIT

2.1 Van Buren County

> Map on the Preceding Page <

SOUTH HAVEN

1 Cheyenne's Closet Vintage Shop

206 Center Street

South Haven
MI 49090

616 637-2955

Memorial Day
to Labor Day:
Daily 9 to 9;

Labor Day to
Dec. 21, and
Feb. 1 to
Memorial Day:
Fri. to Sun.
11 to 7;

Closed Dec. 21
to Feb. 1.

Located in front
of Java Joe's
Espresso Bar,
a block north of
Phoenix Street.

Antique
furniture,
vintage clothing,
jewelry, etc.

JAVA JOE'S

Espresso Bar

Fresh
Bean
Coffee
&
Pastry

Cheyenne's Vintage Closet

Vintage Clothing
Antiques and
Jewelry
Classic Threads
From the
Roaring 20's
to the Hip 70's
WINTER HOURS:
Fri., Sat., Sun. 11-7
(Except for Jam Night)

Both Located at
206 Center St., South Haven
616-637-2955
BUY • SELL • TRADE
Levis • Vintage • Antiques

2   Murphy's Mall

321 Center Street
South Haven MI 49090
616 639-1662
Every day 11 to 5; closed Tues. in winter.
Downtown half block south of Phoenix St.
Crafts, antiques, collectibles;
"Everything under the sun."

Map: City of South Haven:

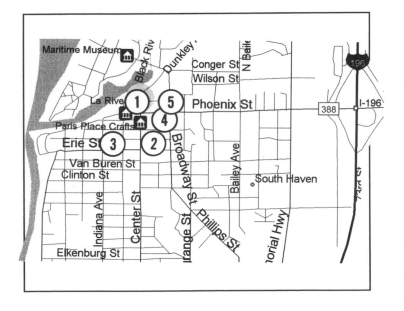

3   Carrousel Mini-Mall
330 South Kalamazoo Street
South Haven   MI 49090
616 639-1501
Wed. to Sun. 10 to 5
South of the main street, west side of the street.
Antique furniture, glassware, nautical items, etc.; also crafts &
custom clothing, and a room full of dolls.

4   Hidden Room Book Shoppe
518 Phoenix Street
South Haven   MI 49090
616 637-7222
May to Aug.: Every day 10 to 5;
Sept. to Dec.: closed Wed.;
Jan. to April: closed Tues. to Thurs.
Downtown, south side of the street.
Antiques and used books.

5   Anchor Antiques Ltd.
527 Phoenix Street
South Haven   MI 49090
616 637-1500
June to Aug.: Mon. through Sat. 10 to 5;
Sept. to Dec.: Fri. Sat. & Sun. 10 to 5;
Closed Jan. Feb. & Mar.;
April & May: Thurs. to Sun. 10 to 5
I-96 Exit 20, at the Welcome Island; west on Phoenix Street
to downtown; north side of the street.
Quality antiques, designer costume jewelry, period furniture
and collectibles, specializing in elegant glass.

6   Sunset Junque Antiques
856 Blue Star Highway
South Haven   MI 49090
616 637-5777
Five miles north of town, west side of the highway.

BANGOR

8   Bangor Antique Mall
215 West Monroe (M-43)
Bangor   MI 49013
616 427-8557
April to Dec.: Mon. to Sat. 10 to 5, Sun. 1 to 5;
Jan. to March: Fri. to Sat. 10 to 5., Sun. 1 to 5
Downtown, south side of the street.
5 Levels, 3 Buildings; large selection of quality antiques.

7   Don Cleveland Auto Museum, Country Store & Antique Shop
65215 M-43 West, four miles out of town
Bangor   MI 49013
616 427-8754
May to Oct.

9   Apple Barn
135 West Monroe
Bangor   MI 49013
No telephone.
Flea market; a few antiques.

LAWRENCE

10   L & R Antiques
50408 Red Arrow Highway
Lawrence   MI 49064
616 674-8562
Sat. & Sun. 10 to 5
1 mile east of Lawrence, north side of the road.
Art glass, furniture and general line.

PAW PAW

11   Antiques & Etc.
237 East Michigan
Paw Paw MI 49079
616 657-4300

12   Paw Paw Antique Gallery
404 East Michigan Avenue
Paw Paw   MI 49079
616 657-5378
Enter parking lot from LaGrave Street, just west of the shop.

13   Country Classics
34026 M-43, at M-40
Paw Paw MI 49079
616 628-0043
Antiques, crafts, used furniture.

LAWTON

14   Old Corner Drugstore & Ice Cream Parlor
156 North Main Street
Lawton   MI 49065
616 624-5261
Ice cream parlor with a few antiques; phasing out of antiques.

MATTAWAN

15   Tom Witte's Antiques
27681 County Road 364 (Front Ave. West)
Mattawan   MI 49071
616 668-4161
Fax: 616 668-5363
Appointment suggested.
Two miles west of downtown, south side of road.
Specializing in antique tools and user tools; also tool auctions.

16   Meadowland Garden Gallery
57636 Murray St.
Mattawan   MI 49071
616 668-5404   Picture frames, gifts, a few antiques.

17   The Livery
57620 Murray Street
Mattawan   MI 49071
616 668-3016
From Halsey Dean Gallery: west on Front Street a block, then
north on Murray Street a half block.   Antiques & gifts.

18   Halsey Dean Gallery
24028 Front Street
Mattawan   MI 49071
616 668-3510
Wed. to Sun. 12 to 5
Downtown, a half mile south of I-94 Exit 66.
Quality furniture and accessories.

HALSEY DEAN GALLERY

**ANTIQUE HOME FURNISHINGS
DEPARTMENT STORE**

24028 Front Street, Mattawan, 616-668-3510

■ **18th & 19th Century American, French, English &
Italian Furniture & Accessories**

■ **Antique China**   ■ **Linens**

■ **Silver**   ■ **Primitives**

19   William Lesterhouse Antiques
24020 Front Street
Mattawan   MI 49071
616 668-3229

GOBLES

20   Holmes Antiques
08757 M-40
Gobles   MI 49055
616 628-2035
Shop may be closing in 1999.

KENDALL

21   Kendall Antiques
26947 County Road 388 ("D" Avenue)
Kendall   MI 49002
616 628-5754
By chance or appointment.
Between Gobles and Highway 131.
Paintings & general line of antiques.

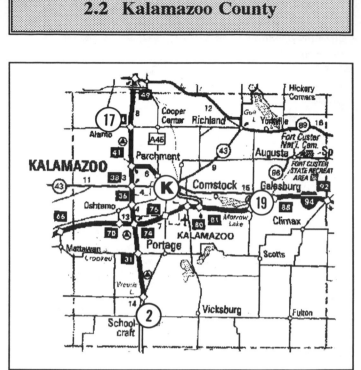

© 1998 AAA - used by permission.

K = City of Kalamazoo: 6 - 15

SCHOOLCRAFT

1   The Antique Gallery
113 North Grand (U.S. 131)
Schoolcraft   MI 49087
616 679-4018

2   Ron's Grand Street Antiques & Mom's Memories
205 North Grand
Schoolcraft   MI 49087
616 679-4774
E-mail: grandst@net-link.net
Tues. to Sat. 10 to 5; Sun. 12 to 5
Downtown, west side of the street.
General line; emphasis on quality, with a sprinkling of unusual
and hard-to-find items.

3   Schoolcraft Antique Mall
209 North Grand
Schoolcraft   MI 49087
616 679-5282; (616 679-4513)

4   Norma's Antiques & Collectibles
231 North Grand
Schoolcraft   MI 49087
616 679-4030

5   Prairie Home Antiques
240 North Grand (U.S. 131)
Schoolcraft   MI 49087
616 679-2062 or 877 679-2062

KALAMAZOO

Map: City of Kalamazoo:

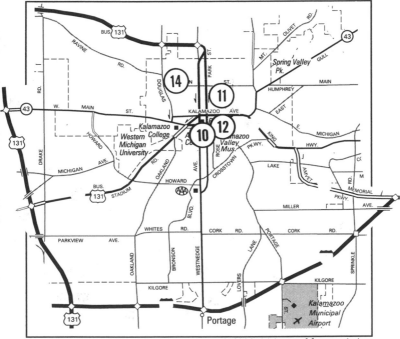

© 1998 AAA - used by permission.

6   Attic Trash & Treasures
1301 South Westnedge, at Forest Street
Kalamazoo   MI 49008
616 344-2189
Used furniture and antiques.

7   Pennyrose
906 South Westnedge, south of Forest Street
Kalamazoo MI 49008
616 381-8747
Art and some antiques.

8   Aaron & Associates
824 South Westnedge, near Vine Street
Kalamazoo   MI 49008   616 342-8834

9   Lade Das
426 South Burdick
Kalamazoo MI 49008
616 342-6759   Vintage clothing.

10   JP's Coins & Collectibles
420 South Burdick
Kalamazoo MI 49007
616 383-2200
Mon. to Sat. 10 to 5
Downtown, west side of the street, one block south of the State Theater.
Coins, collectibles, antiques, fashion jewelry.

11   The Emporium
313 East Kalamazoo Avenue
Kalamazoo   MI 49007
616 381-0998
Mon. to Fri. 7 p.m. to 9 p.m., Sat. & Sun. 2 to 6
Downtown; northeast corner Kalamazoo & Pitcher.
18,000 square feet of furniture, 1,000 pieces on hand.

12   Kalamazoo Antiques Market
130 North Edwards St.
Kalamazoo MI 49007
616 226-9788

Mon. to Fri. 11 to 6,
Sat. 10 to 6,
Sun. 1 to 5

U.S. 131 Exit 36 east;
I-94 Exit 78 north;
Michigan Ave. to
Edwards.

East side of Edwards
Street between East
Michigan Ave. &
East Kalamazoo Ave.

Kalamazoo Antiques Market

130 NORTH EDWARDS STREET
KALAMAZOO, MI 49007 616-226-9788

Multi-dealer market in the heart of downtown Kalamazoo, offers a broad variety of fine quality antiques: Primitives to Victorian to Fifties
HOURS: MON.-FRI. 11 AM-6PM
SAT. 10 AM-6PM, SUN. 1PM-5PM

Directions: From US 131: Exit 36 East to downtown. From I-94: Exit 78 N. to downtown Michigan Ave. to Edwards (behind Wendy's)

A good quality antique
market.

13   Heritage Architectural Salvage
150 North Edwards
Kalamazoo   MI 49000
616 385-1004

14   Brook Farm General Market
3006 Douglas, north of Business 131
Kalamazoo   MI 49004
616 342-6551
Antiques and new & used furniture.

15   Red Wagon Antiques
5348 North Riverview, north of G Avenue
Kalamazoo   MI 49004
616 382-5461

PARACHMENT

16   Welborn Antiques
6300 North Riverview, north of McKinley
Parchment MI 49004
616 345-3665

ALAMO

17   Alamo Depot Antique Mall
6187 West "D" Avenue
Alamo (Kalamazoo)   MI 49009
616 373-3885; Fax: 616 373-7048
Mon. to Thurs.: 10 to 6; Fri. & Sat. 10 to 8; Sun. 12 to 6
South side of road, 1/2 mile west of U.S. 131 Exit 44.
Quality oak furniture, glassware and accessories.   9,600
square foot multi-dealer mall, credit cards accepted.
Visit the Club Car Restaurant and Alamo Depot Craft Mall
in the same building.

COOPER CENTER

18 Last Chance Antiques
8120 Douglas Avenue, between C and D Avenues
Cooper Center (Kalamazoo)   MI 49004
616 381-5573; E-Mail: RCARL@compuserve.com
Former gas station.

GALESBURG

19 Grant's Antique Market
33 West Battle Creek Street
Galesburg   MI 49053
616 665-4300
From west on I-94 use Exit 85;
from the east use Exit 88.

2.3 Calhoun County

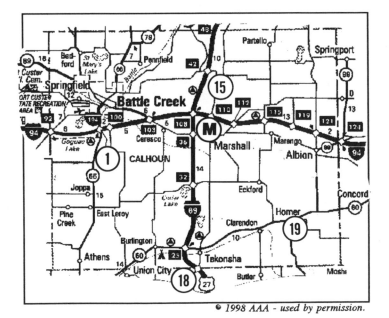

© 1998 AAA - used by permission.

M = City of Marshall: 3 - 14

BATTLE CREEK

1   Karen's Keepsakes Antique Mall
4359 Capitol Avenue
Battle Creek MI 49015
616 979-1800
Mon. to Sat. 10 to 5
1.6 miles south of I-94, east side of road.   Park and enter in the rear.
Gifts, primitives, Steiff bears, Victorian, jewelry, quilts, furniture, glassware, and new Fenton Art Glass.

2   Timeless Treasures
548 Capital Ave. S.W.
Battle Creek MI 49015
616 964-6341; Used furniture, collectibles, some antiques.

MARSHALL

3   Heirlooms Unlimited
211 West Michigan Avenue
Marshall   MI 49068
616 781-1234

4   Pineapple Lane Antiques
209 West Michigan Avenue
Marshall   MI 49068
616 789-1445
Mon. to Sat. 11 to 5, Sun. 12 to 5
Downtown, south side of the street.
General line of antiques; also Boyd & Ganz Cottage Collectibles.

5   J & J Antiques and Tea Room
206 West Michigan Avenue
Marshall   MI 49068
616 781-5581;   tea room, gifts, antiques.

6   Little Toy Drum Antiques
135 West Michigan Avenue
Marshall   MI 49068
616 781-9644;   gifts and antiques.

7   Baldwin Antiques
127 1/2 West Michigan Avenue, lower level
Marshall   MI 49068
616 781-2678

8   Finders Keepers
125 1/2 West Michigan Avenue, lower level
Marshall   MI 49068
616 789-1611

9   HilDor House Antiques
105 West Michigan Avenue
Marshall   MI 49068
616 789-0009
This shop is scheduled to close early 1999.

10   J.H. Cronin Antique Center
101 West Michigan Avenue
Marshall   MI 49068
616 789-0077
Mon. to Sat. 10 to 6 (Jan. & Feb. until 5); Sun. 12 to 5
Downtown Marshall, which is the city where I-94 and I-69
intersect. Located in National Historic Landmark District.
Toys, banks, advertising, furniture, glass, etc.
All items guaranteed - no reproductions.

11   Keystone Antiques
110 East Michigan Avenue
Marshall MI 49068
616 789-1355.
Wed. to Fri. 1 to 5, Sat. 10 to 5, Sun. 1 to 5
Downtown
Architectural and general antiques, and new & old concrete
garden statuary.

12   Smithfield Banques
117 East Michigan Avenue
Marshall   MI 49068
616 781-6969

13   Marshall House Antique Centre
100 Exchange Street
Marshall   MI 49068
616 781-7841
Mon. to Sat. 11 to 5, Sun. 12 to 5
Just off the main street next to a little park, east edge of
downtown, in a beautiful old mansion.
14 dealers.   Quality Victorian antiques, specializing in walnut;
also Haviland China, primitives, etc.

MARSHALL HOUSE ANTIQUE CENTRE
100 Exchange St. • Marshall, MI. • (616)781-7841
OPEN: MON-SAT 11 to 5 • SUN 12 to 5

14   McKee Monument & Mercantile
201 Exchange Street
Marshall   MI 49068
616 781-8921
Daily 11 to 5:30, Sun. 12 to 5:30, closed Wed. & Thurs.
Downtown at East Green & Exchange Streets, a block south
of Michigan Street.
Country store setting; advertising, toys, dolls, books, & vintage
clothing.

15   Country House Antiques
19724 North Old U.S. 27
Marshall   MI 49068
616 781-2046
Call first, or by chance.
6 miles north of Marshall on Old U.S. 27, east side of road
just north of "N" Drive.
Country furniture, finished & in the rough, & country
accessories; also herbs & dried flowers.

TURKEYVILLE

16   The Olde Homestead Antique Mall
15445 N Drive North (Turkeyville Road)
Turkeyville (Marshall)   MI 49068
616 781-8119
Northeast corner N Drive North & 15 1/2 Mile Road, one
half mile west of I-69 Exit 42.

17   Bushong's Antiques
18600 16 Mile Road
Turkeyville (Marshall)   MI 49068
616 781-5832
Exit 42 of I-69, west 1/8 mile to 16 mile road, south on 16
mile road.   Shop is in a stone house on east side of road.

TEKONSHA

18   Kempton's Country Classics
1129 Marshall Road South (Old U.S. 27)
Tekonsha   MI 49092
517 279-8130
Tues. to Sat. 10 to 5
5 miles south of Tekonsha, west side of road.
Early American furniture, primitives, folk art, etc.

HOMER

19   Bailey's Antiques
102 East Main Street
Homer MI 49245
517 568-4014
Fri. & Sat. & Mon. 10 to 6, Sun. 12 to 6, or by chance or
appointment.
A block south of the water tower at M-60 & Sophia.
Early American Pattern Glass, Americana, steins, etc.

SUGGESTION TO TRAVELERS:

The next time you must drive across the state between the
Chicago-Niles area and the Detroit-Jackson area, forget
boring Interstate Highway 94!

Instead, take scenic, interesting, and more direct Michigan
Highway 60.

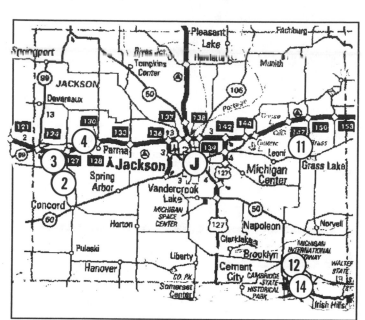

© 1998 AAA - used by permission.

J = City of Jackson: 5 - 9

CONCORD

1   Fuzzy's Old Toys
12123 Spring Arbor Road (M-60 East)
Concord   MI 49237
517 524-9027
Mon. to Sat. 10 to 6, Sun. 12 to 6
Old toys and a general line of antiques.

2   King Road Granary
12700 King Road
Concord MI 49237
517 524-6006
April to Nov. 15: Daily 10 to 6
South from I-94 Exit 127 on West Concord Road 3.5 miles to
King Road, west 1/2 mile; barn in back of house, north side
of road.
General line of antiques.

PARMA

3   Harley's Antique Mall
13789 Donovan Road
Parma   MI 49224
517 531-5300
Open 10 to 8 364 Days a Year.
I-94 Exit 127, southwest corner.
Michigan's most friendly mall! Open until 8 p.m. 364 days a
year! Save up to 40% at the on-site bookstore, offering
Michigan's widest selection of antique price guides, historical
Dover Reprints, history of fashion and architecture books.
European specialty food store on site too.

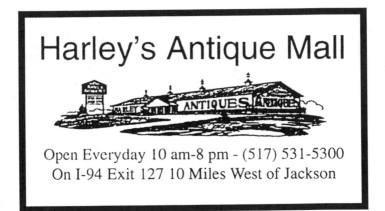

Harley's Antique Mall

Open Everyday 10 am-8 pm - (517) 531-5300
On I-94 Exit 127 10 Miles West of Jackson

4   Cracker Hill Antique Mall
12000 Norton Road
Parma   MI 49269
517 531-4200
Mon. to Sat. 10 to 6; Sun. 12 to 6
Exit 128, north side of I-94.
40 + dealers.   Animal & fish mounts, fishing lures, tin & cast
iron toys, etc. In business since 1984.

JACKSON

5   Treasureable Finds
145 North Jackson Street
Jackson   MI 49201
517 768-1120;   May be moving in 1999.

Map: City of Jackson:

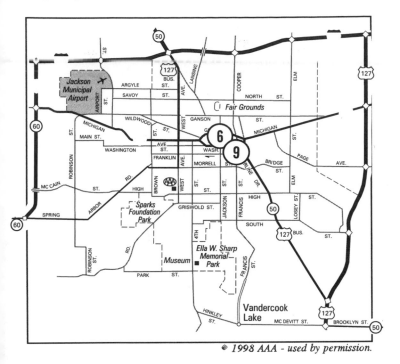

⊕ 1998 AAA - used by permission.

6 The Jackson Antique Mall
201 North Jackson Street
Jackson   MI 49201
517 784-3333
Mon. to Sat.: 10 to 6, Sun. 12 to 5
Northeast corner Pearl & Jackson Streets, downtown.
40 dealers.

7 Ann's Copper Brass & Glass
218 South Mechanic
Jackson   MI 49201
517 782-8817

8 Second Hand Rose
129 East Michigan Avenue
Jackson   MI 49201
517 789-8239
Art deco, jewelry, and a general line of antiques.

9 The Camp Gallery
109 West Washington
Jackson MI 49201
517 780-0606; 800 962-5038
Mon. to Sat. 9 to 6; Sun. call ahead; closed Holidays.
Downtown, on east-bound Business Route 94.
15,000 square feet; antiques, collectibles, crafts.

VANDERCOOK

10 Loretta Lynn's
1361 East McDevitt, U.S. 127 & M-50
Vandercook (Jackson) MI 49203
517 782-5101
Furniture & housewares; some antiques.

GRASS LAKE

11 Grand Illusion Gallery & Architectural Salvage
201 East & 103 West Michigan
Grass Lake MI 48240
517 522-8715
Mon. to Sat. 10 to 4, Sun. 12 to 4; closed Sun. in winter.
I-94 Exit 150 south 3.1 miles. Downtown, south side of street.
Architectural salvage, art, jewelry.

BROOKLYN

Note: Several shops with a Brooklyn address are located in Lenawee County.

12   Pinetree Centre Antique Mall
129 North Main Street
Brooklyn MI 49230
517 592-3808
Daily 10 to 5; Sun. 12 to 6
Downtown, east side of the Square.
General line of antiques.

13   Brooklyn Depot / Brosamer's Bells
207 Irwin Street
Brooklyn MI 49230
517 592-6885
Office furniture and bells.

14   Memory Lane Antiques
12939 South M-50
Brooklyn MI 49230
517 592-4218
Every day 10:30 to 6
One mile northwest of U.S. 12, across from Michigan Speedway.
Milk bottles, pottery, oak furniture, toys.   Also: a Dairy Museum.

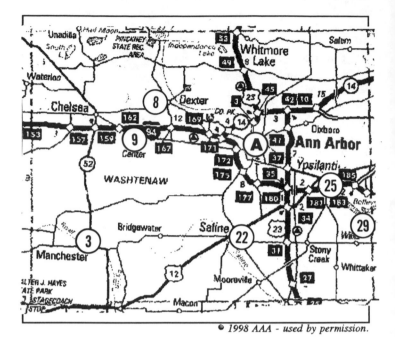

© 1998 AAA - used by permission.

MANCHESTER

1   Manchester Antique Mall
116 East Main Street
Manchester MI 48158
734 428-9357

2   The 18th Century Shoppe
122 East Main Street
Manchester MI 48158
734 428-7759   Countryware, herbs, gifts; a few antiques.

3   Limpert Antiques
201 East Main Street, lower level Manchester Mill
Manchester MI 48158
734 428-7400 (Leave message)
Open by appointment only, or by chance.
Civil War, advertising, primitives etc.

4   Raisin Valley Antiques
201 East Main Street, in the Mill
Manchester MI 48158
734 428-7766; res. 734 428-8518

CHELSEA

5   Uptown Antiques & Littlewares
Sylvan Building, 114 North Main Street
Chelsea MI 48118   734 475-6940

6   Chelsea Woodwork & Antiques
407 North Main Street, just north of the tracks
Chelsea MI 48118   734 475-8020

7   Darwin's Studio
9080 Beeman Road
Chelsea MI 48118
734 475-9730   Stained Glass, antiques & slot machines.

DEXTER

8 Designer's Cove
3127 Baker Road
Dexter MI 48130
734 426-2688
Daily 10 to 5:30, Sat. 10 to 2, closed Wed. & Sun.
Several miles north of I-94, west side of road.
Upholstery shop with some reupholstered antiques for sale.

8.5   Johnson's Antique Shop
11511 Jackson Road
Dexter MI 48130   734 475-1902

9   Glenbrier Antiques
351 North Dancer Road
Dexter MI 48130
734 475-2961
Every Day 10 to 6
Quarter mile north of Jackson Road; use Exit 162 from I-94
eastbound, and Exit 167 from I-94 westbound.
Two shops: His: vintage tools; Hers: glass, general line.

ANN ARBOR

10   The Lotus Gallery
1570 Covington Drive
Ann Arbor MI 48103   734 665-6322

11   Rage Of The Age
314 South Ashley Street, between Wayne and Liberty
Ann Arbor MI 48107
734 662-0777

Map of Ann Arbor:

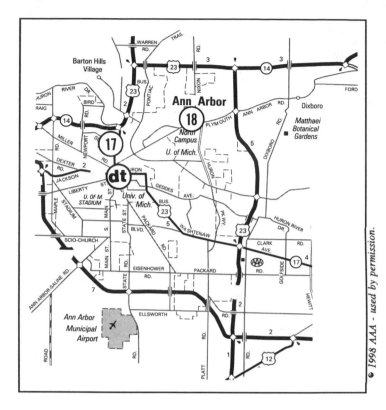

dt = Downtown Ann Arbor: 10 - 16

12   Barclay Gallery
218 South Main, between Liberty and Washington
Ann Arbor MI 48104
734 663-2900

13   Arcadian Too
118 South Main Street
Ann Arbor MI 48104
734 994-8856
Mon. to Thurs. 11 to 6, Fri. 11 to 9, Sat. 10 to 9, Sun. 12 to 6
Downtown, west side the street, south of Washington.
Antique furniture, depression glass, sterling, Flo Blue, and
jewelry.   Good quality shop.

14   Past Presence Antiques
303 South Division, at Liberty
Ann Arbor MI 48104
734 663-2352
European & American antiques.

15   Arcadian Antiques & Collectibles
13-15 Nickels Arcade
Ann Arbor MI 48104
734 994-3433
Mon. to Sat. 10 to 5, Sun. 11 to 5
The historic Arcade is located on the east side of Maynard
Street between William and Liberty Streets.
Antique purses, cameo, ink wells, hand painted plates, pocket
watches.

16   The Treasure Mart
529 Detroit Street, between Fifth and Division
Ann Arbor MI 48104
734 662-9887
Three floors of household goods and antiques on
consignment.

17   MacGregor's Outdoors, Inc.
803 North Main
Ann Arbor MI 48107
734 761-9200; Fax: 734 761-9204
Mon. to Sat. 10 to 6
Northwest corner Main & Summit, one mile south of M-14.
Parking in back off Summit.
Fine European and American antique furniture.
In addition to antique furniture, MacGregor's is a full-line
Orvis fly fishing dealer.

18   Antiques Mall of Ann Arbor
2739 Plymouth Road, in Plymouth Road Shopping Center
Ann Arbor MI 48105
734 663-8200
*Note: Big Two-Hearted, formerly located in Charlevoix, now
sells Arts & Crafts style antiques from a booth in the Antiques
Mall of Ann Arbor.   The mall is open Mon. to Sat. 11 to 7,
Sun. 12 to 5*

SALINE

19   Antique International Interiors
405 North Ann Arbor Street
Saline MI 48176
734 944-3500
Interiors; only a few antiques.

20   The Drowsy Parrot
105 North Ann Arbor
Saline MI 48176
734 429-8595   Restaurant with a few antiques.

Map of Saline:

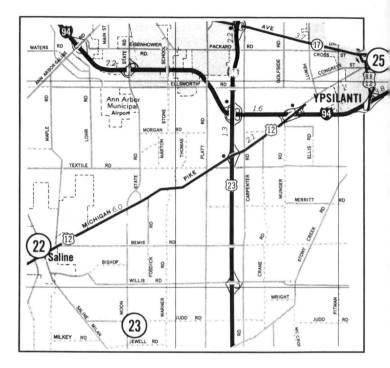

21   Pineapple House Interiors
101 East Michigan
Saline MI 48176
734 429-1174
Interior design, decorative items, new furniture, some
antiques.

22   Salt City Antiques
116 West Michigan Avenue (U.S. Highway 12)
Saline MI 48176
734 429-3997
Mon. to Sat. 10 to 5, Sun. 11 to 5
Downtown, north side of street.
12 dealers. Furniture, glassware, pottery, vintage clothing,
50's collectibles, Victorian items, primitives, etc.
Also: a collection of Blue Ridge Dinnerware, and Shelley
Bone China.

23   Attic Treasures Antiques
10360 Moon Road, between Judd & Jewel
Saline MI 48176
734 429-4242

YPSILANTI

24   Schmidt's Antiques
5138 West Michigan
Ypsilanti MI 48197
734 434-2660

25   Materials Unlimited
2 West Michigan Avenue
Ypsilanti MI 48197
800 299-9462; Fax 734 482-3636
www.mat-unl.com
Mon. to Sat. 10 to 5
Downtown, north side of street just west of the river.
15,000 square feet of antiques and architecturals. Lighting,
mantels, furniture, glass and more.

26   Silver Spoon Antiques
27 East Cross, Depot Town
Ypsilanti MI 48197
734 484-9960
Estate jewelry, glassware, furniture, and more.

Map: City of Ypsilanti:

© 1998 AAA - used by permission.

27   Jim MacDonald's Antiques &
Apple Annies Vintage Clothing
29 East Cross Street
Ypsilanti MI 48198
734 481-0555

28   McFarlane Antiques
10970 Ford Road (M-153)
Ypsilanti MI 48197
734 482-1307
From Exit 10 of M-14 go east on M-153 4 miles.

29   Schmidt Antique Village
7099 McKean Road
Ypsilanti MI 48197
734 485-8606
Thurs. to Mon. 11 to 5
From I-94 Exit 187 south on Rawsonville Road one mile to
Textile, west to McKean, then south one mile.
General line of antiques, plus auctions.

30   Pegasus Antiques
7700 Currie Road
Salem
248 348-6652
Scheduled to open early 1999.

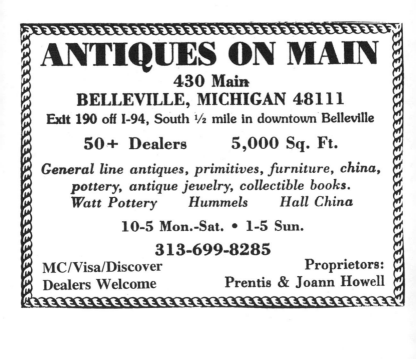

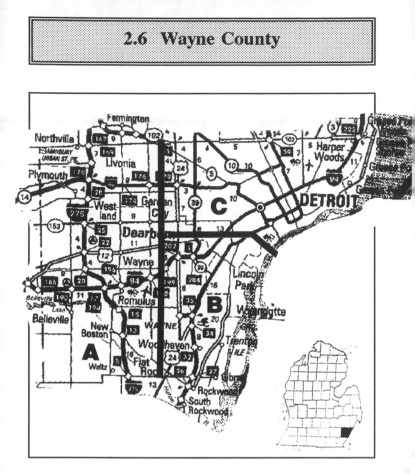

Districts within Wayne County:

A: Western Wayne County
B: Southern Wayne County
C: Eastern Wayne County

A. Western Wayne County

BELLEVILLE

1   Antiques on Main
430 Main Street
Belleville   MI 48111
734 699-8285
Mon. to Sat. 10 to 5, Sun. 1 to 5
Exit 190 from I-94, south 1/2 mile in downtown Belleville.
East side of the street.
General line antiques, primitives, furniture, china, pottery, books.

ROMULUS

2   Udders Nostalgia Shop
36628 Goddard Road
Romulus MI 48174
734 941-1465

WAYNE

3   Sanders Antiques
35118 W. Michigan (West-bound lanes, west of Wayne Road.)
Wayne MI 48184
734 721-3029
Every day 10 to 6

4   Heritage Colonial Upholstering & Antiques
32224 Michigan Avenue, between Meriman & Menoy
Wayne MI 48184
734 722-2332

5   Blue Willow
34840 West Michigan (West-bound lanes.)
Wayne MI 48184
734 729-4910
Mon. to Sat. 11 to 6
North side of street, 1 block east of Wayne Road.
Pottery and a general line of antiques.

GARDEN CITY

6   Craftique Craft & Antiques Mall
5846 Middlebelt
Garden City MI 48135
734 525-9900
www.craftique.com
In Garden City Town Center Mall, at Ford Road.

WESTLAND

7   Antiques & Collectibles
38411 Joy Road
Westland MI 48185
734 254-9581
www.beaniesoldhere.com
Mon. to Sat. 10 to 8; Thanksgiving to Christmas: 9 to 9
Joy-Hix Shopping Plaza, east of I-275.
"Primitives to the present."   Beanie babies, sports, dolls,
glassware, Princess Di collectibles.

Map: Western Wayne County:

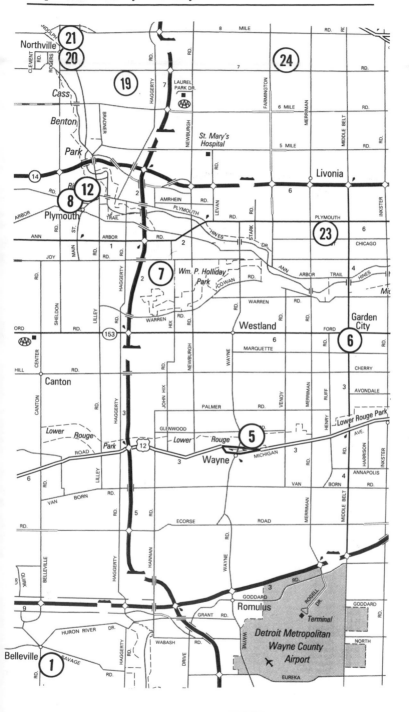

PLYMOUTH

8   The Plymouth Antique Mall
975 West Ann Arbor Trail
Plymouth MI 48170
734 459-0000; 734 451-7444
Mon. to Sat. 10 to 5, Sun. 12 to 5
Downtown, between Main & Harvey Streets.
Glassware, furniture, quilts, general line.

9   Memory Lane Antiques
336 South Main, north of Ann Arbor Trail
Plymouth MI 48170
734 451-1873

10   Jack's Corner Bookstore
583 West Ann Arbor Trail
Plymouth MI 48170
734 455-2373

Map: City of Plymouth:

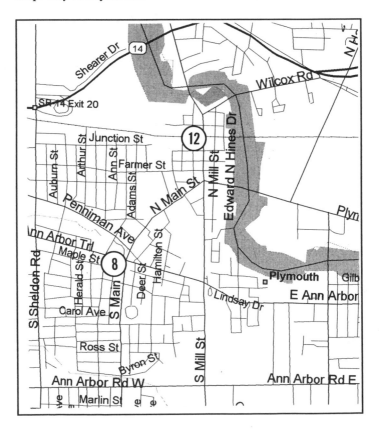

11   The Michael Camp Shoppe
331 North Main Street, just north of the tracks
Plymouth MI 48170
734 453-0367

12   Bellerose
643 North Mill Street
Plymouth MI 48170
734 454-5510
Bellerose7@media1.net
Daily 11 to 6, Fri. to 8
Three blocks north of Plymouth Road.
General line.

13   Robin's Nest Antiques
640 Starkweather
Plymouth MI 48170
734 459-7733
Old Village area, half block east of Liberty Street.

14   Kalik's Antiques
198 West Liberty
Plymouth MI 48170
734 455-5595;   KALIKANTIQ@aol.com

15   In My Attic
157 West Liberty Street (Moved from 865 Wing)
Plymouth MI 48170
734 455-8970

16   Upstairs, Downstairs Antiques
149 West Liberty
Plymouth MI 48170
734 459-6450

■ NORTHVILLE ■

17   The Barn Antiques
48120 West 8 Mile Road
Northville MI 48167
248 349-0117

18   Morrison's Antiques
105 East Main Street
Northville MI 48167
248 348-8898

19   Knightsbridge Antique Mall
42305 West 7 Mile Road
Northville MI 48167
248 344-7200
Daily 11 to 6, Wed. to 8
Two miles west of I-275, in strip mall, south side of the road.
High quality mall; 26,000 sq. ft., 200 dealers.

KNIGHTSBRIDGE ANTIQUES

**42305 W. 7 Mile Rd. • Northville, MI 48167
(248) 344-7200**

*Michigan's Largest High Quality Antique Shop
26,000 Sq. Ft., Over 200 Dealers*

*Located just west of Detroit, only 20 min. from
Greenfield Village,
Henry Ford Museum and Metro Airport*

4 other multi-dealer shops within 10 miles

New merchandise arriving daily

**2 miles West of I-275
Exit 169**

20   The Hopeless Romantic
156 North Center
Northville MI 48167
248 374-9124
Mon. to Sat. 10 to 5, Sun. 12 to 3
One block north of the downtown light, Center & Dunlap,
behind florist shop. Entrance through the florist shop or from
public parking lot in back, off Dunlap Street.
Eclectic mix, including Victorian and items with a floral
theme.

21   Sherwood Picture Framing and Antiques Ltd.
111 East Main Street
Northville MI 48167
248 347-4890
Tues. to Fri. 10 to 6, Sat. 10 to 5, Mon. by chance.
Downtown, north side of the street.
Quality antiques, including furniture, pottery, etc, and picture
framing service.

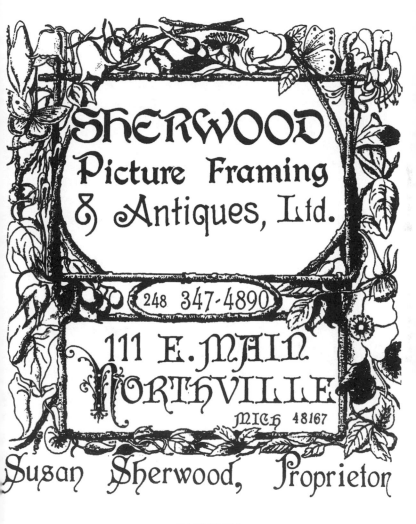

SHERWOOD Picture Framing & Antiques, Ltd.

248 347-4890

111 E. MAIN NORTHVILLE MICH 48167

Susan Sherwood, Proprietor

LIVONIA

22   Countryside Craft Mall & Antiques
35323 Plymouth Road, west of Wayne Road
Livonia MI 48150
734 513-2577

23 Town & Country Antiques Mall
31630 Plymouth Road
Livonia MI 48150
734 425-4344
Mon. Tues. Wed. & Sun. 11 to 6, Thurs. to Sat. 11 to 8
1 block west of Merriman Road, 1 mile south of I-96, behind
East Side Mario's Restaurant.
55 dealers.   Depression Glass, furniture, sports memorabilia,
jewelry, etc.

24 Now 'N' Then
33200 Seven Mile Road
Livonia MI 48152
248 476-0055
Tue. to Sat. 11 to 5, Sun. 12 to 4
North side of the Street, 2 blocks east of Farmington Road.
Gifts, jewelry, collectibles, antiques.

B: Southern Wayne County

TRENTON

25 Don's Antiques & Collectibles
2857 West Jefferson, south of West Road
Trenton MI 48183
734 676-0622

WYANDOTTE

26 Bargain City & Antiques
3274 Fort, north of Stewart
Wyandotte MI 48192

27 Tony's Junk Shop   (Pawn shop)
1325 Fort, between North Line & Goddard
Wyandotte MI 48192
734 283-2160

28 J & J Antiques
1836 Biddle
Wyandotte MI 48192
734 283-6019
Tues. to Sat. 9 to 6
West side of highway, north of North Line Road.
20 dealers; general line with furniture, glassware, dolls, etc.
New merchandise arriving daily.

Map: Southern Wayne County:

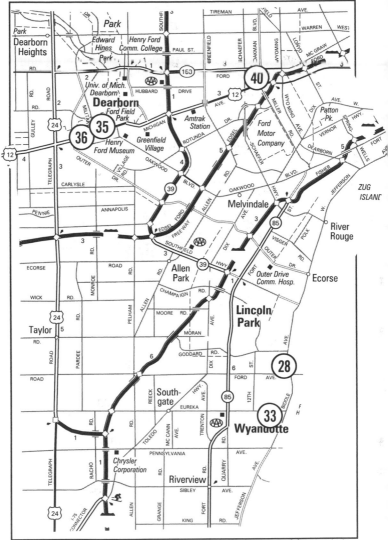

© 1998 AAA - used by permission.

29   Raggedy Dan's
1842 Biddle
Wyandotte MI 48192
734 283-3370

30   Almost Antique
1728 Eureka Road
Wyandotte MI 48192
734 285-0477

31   Old Gray House Antiques
303 Oak Street
Wyandotte MI 48192
734 285-2555

32   Yesterday's Treasures
258 Elm Street
Wyandotte MI 48192
734 283-5232

33   Armstrong's Antiques & Collectibles
2912 Biddle Street
Wyandotte MI 48192
734 282-3072
Mon. to Sat. 10 to 5, closed Wed. & Sun.
Downtown, southwest corner Oak & Biddle.
String instruments, Barbies/dolls, glassware, sports/fishing,
furniture, toys/games, linens, fine collectibles.

LINCOLN PARK

34   Mr. Robinson's Resale
4145 Dix Highway, between North Line and Goddard
Lincoln Park MI 48146
313 382-1600

DEARBORN

35   Howard Street Antiques Coop
921 Howard Street, east of Military, north of Michigan
Dearborn MI 48124
313 563-9352

36   Village Antique Mall
22630 Michigan Avenue
Dearborn MI 48124
313 563-1230
Mon. to Sat. 10:30 to 5:30; Sun. 12 to 5; Thurs open to 7:30
One block west of Military, north side of the street.
Antiques, collectibles, jewelry, advertising, military, toys.

37   Comer-Copia
21903 Michigan Avenue, at Oakwood
Dearborn MI 48124,   313 565-0875

38   Retro Image
14246 Michigan Avenue, between Schaffer & Greenfield
Dearborn MI 48126   313 582-3074

39   Desirable Discs II
13357 Michigan Avenue, west of Maple
Dearborn MI 48126
313 581-1767

40   A & D Antiques
13354 Michigan Avenue
Dearborn MI 48126
313 581-6183
Mon. to Fri 10 to 7, Sat. 10 to 4
One block east of Schaffer, north side of the street.
Fine art, oriental rugs, and general antiques.

C: Eastern Wayne County

DETROIT

41   Team Antiques
19403 West Warren, east of Evergreen
Detroit MI 48228
313 336-2121

42   New World Antique Gallery
12101 Grand River, at Washington
Detroit MI 48204
313 834-7008
Antiques and used furniture, much of it in the rough.

43   Michigan Avenue Antiques
7105 Michigan Avenue
Detroit MI 48210
313 554-1012

44   Xavier's
2546 Michigan Avenue, west of Tiger Stadium
Detroit MI 48216
313 964-1222   Arts & Crafts, Art Deco, etc.

45   Detroit Antique Mall & Senate Resale
828 West Fisher Freeway
Detroit MI 48201
313 963-5252
Tues. to Sat. 11 to 6
Northwest of downtown. North side of entrance ramp to
Fisher Freeway, just west of Grand River Avenue. (There is a
street to avoid entering the freeway after leaving the mall.)
Large interesting mixture of antiques and used furniture.

Map: Eastern Wayne County:

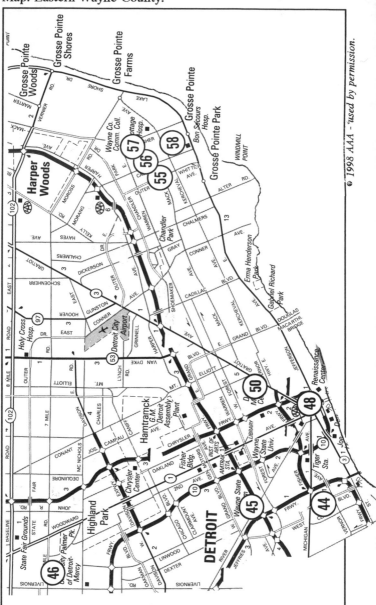

46   Gilbert's Antiques & Fine Furniture

19150 Livernois Ave.
Detroit MI 48221
313 340-1611
Tues. to Sat. 12 to 6:30 or by appointment.
A block north of Seven Mile Road, east side of the street.
Furniture from the late 1800's to the early 20th Century.

47   John K. King Books
901 West Lafayette Boulevard, west of Lodge Expressway
Detroit MI 48226
313 961-0622   E-mail: kingbooks@aol.com
Huge used book store, plus some antiques.

48   DuMouchelle Art Gallery
409 East Jefferson, across from Renaissance Center
Detroit MI 48226
313 963-6255

49   Dell Pryor Galleries
1452 Randolph, in the Harmonie Park Historic District.
Detroit MI 48226
313 963-5977
Contemporary art & good quality antiques.

50   Marketplace Antiques
2047 Gratiot, at St. Alban Street
Detroit MI 48207
313 567-8250

51   Villa Domain
8469 East Jefferson, in the historic Indian Village area
Detroit MI 48214
313 824-4600

52   Harper Galleries
8445 East Jefferson
Detroit MI 48214
313 821-1952

53   William Charles Gallery
8025 East Agnes, east of Van Dyke
Detroit MI 48214   313 823-0324

54   Mike's Antiques
11109 Morang, west of I-94 Cadieux exit
Detroit MI 48224   313 881-9500

55   London Galleries
16231 Mack Avenue
Detroit   MI 48224
313 882-4776
Mon. to Sat. 11 to 6, Sun. 12 to 6
North side of the street, at Three Mile Road, 3 blocks west of
Outer Drive.
17 dealers; 18th Century furniture, nautical items, art deco,
retro 60's, folk art, etc.

56   Park Antiques
16235 Mack Avenue
Detroit   MI 48224
313 884-7652
Wed. to Sat. 12 to 5
North side of street, west of Three Mile Road.
General line of quality antiques.

57   Another Time
16239 Mack Avenue
Detroit   MI 48224
313 886-0830
Wed. to Sat. 11 to 6
North side of street, west of Three Mile Road.
Lighting fixtures, mahogany furniture, African art, etc.

GROSSE POINTE PARK

58   Lloyd David Antiques
15302 Kercheval
Grosse Pointe Park   MI 48230
313 822-3452
Mon. & Wed. to Sat. 11 to 6
One mile west of Cadieux, south side of street.
Antique furniture, American art pottery, fine used furniture,
and collectibles.

59   Birds of a Feather
15227 Kercheval, west of Beaconfield
Grosse Pointe Park   MI 48230
313 331-1666

GROSSE POINTE

60   Charterhouse & Co
16835 Kercheval, east of Cadieux
Grosse Pointe City   MI 48230
313 885-1232

GROSSE POINTE WOODS

61   Calling House Antiques
20788 Mack, north of Vernier
Grosse Pointe Woods   MI 48236
313 882-1652

TIER 3:
SAUGATUCK-LANSING-ROYAL OAK

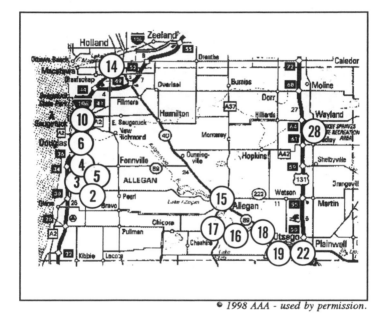

© 1998 AAA - used by permission.

GLENN

1   Helen's Antiques
1662 Adams Road (Blue Star Highway), east of I-196
Glenn   MI 49416
616 227-3211

2   Willow Bend Antiques
1671 Blue Star Highway
Glenn MI 49408
616 227-3200
Summer: Fri. to Mon. 11 to 5;
Winter: Sat. & Sun. 11 to 5
East of I-196, Exit 34, east side of highway.
General line of antiques.

DOUGLAS

Map: Saugatuck - Douglas area:

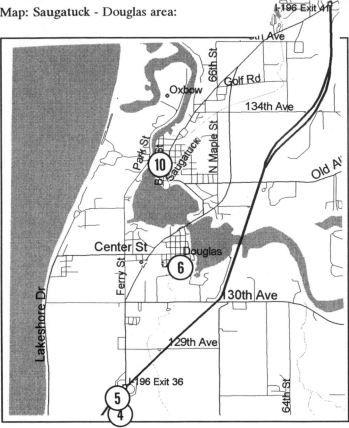

3   Bird Cage Antiques
Blue Star Highway & M-89.
Saugatuck/Douglas Area MI 49408
616 543-4732
Summer: Open Daily 12 to 6
I-196 Exit 34, east a block to blinker light, then south at Shell
Station one block; west side of street.
Large warehouse full of dining room sets, European furniture,
etc. Large selection of chandeliers.

4   White Birch Trading
2788 Blue Star Highway
Saugatuck/Douglas Area MI 49453
616 857-7474
July & August: Thurs. to Mon. 11 to 5;
Other times: call for hours or for appointment.
I-196 Exit 36, then 300 feet south; west side of the highway.
Antiques, reproductions, garden collectibles.

5   Tim's Treasures
2790 Blue Star Highway
Douglas MI 49406
616 857-7157
Summer: Mon. to Sat. 11 to 6, Sun. 12 to 6, closed Wed.;
Winter: Nice weekends and by appointment.
I-196 Exit 36, then south a block.
16 dealers; variety of merchandise.

6   Olde House Antiques
112 Center Street
Douglas   MI 49406
616 857-1623
Memorial Day to Labor Day: Every Day 11 to 6
Downtown
Historic 1872 house; Victorian furniture, & some new items.

7   Edwards Limited
36 Center Street
Douglas MI 49406
616 857-1977   Closed winters.

8   Rabbit Run Art & Antiques
33 Center Street
Douglas MI 49406
616 857-5174

SAUGATUCK

9   Country Store Antiques
120 Butler Street
Saugatuck   MI 49453
616 857-8601; if no answer call 616 396-1841

10   Swell Times
421 Water Street
Saugatuck   MI 49453
616 857-8320
Summer: Daily 11 to 6, later Fri. & Sat.;   Winter: call for
hours.
Across the road from the water.
Deco thru 70's.

11   Evergreen Cottage Antiques
3277 Blue Star Highway
Saugatuck   MI 49453
616 857-5817

12   Centennial Antiques
3421 Holland Road
Saugatuck   MI 49453
616 857-2743

13   Andy's Antiques
3400 block Blue Star Highway
Saugatuck   MI 49403

HOLLAND

*Note: Most of the shops and malls in Holland are in Ottawa
County, Section 4.1.*

14   Nob Hill Antique Mall
1261 Graafschap Road (i.e. 60th Street)
Holland (Graafschap) MI 49423
616 392-1424
Mon. to Sat. 10 to 5:30
A mile south of 32nd Street & a mile west of Business 31, at
146th Avenue
Thirty dealers, 130 year old building.

ALLEGAN

15   Water Street Place Mall Antiques Etc.
420 Water Street
Allegan MI 49010
616 673-5841
Winter: Fri., Sat., & Mon. 10 to 5, Sun. 12 to 5;
Extended hours come Spring.
North end of beautiful historic Downtown Allegan.
Primitives to 50's: glassware, furniture, books, linens, jewelry,
toys, dolls, and a Christmas Closet.

16   Dawn's Antique Barn
1259 Williams Bridge Road
Allegan   MI 49010
616 673-2253, 616 521-7529
Daily 10 to 5, closed Thurs., Sun. by chance.
South one mile on M-89 to Williams Bridge Road, south 1/2
mile, east side of road.
Pottery, glass, china, comics, records, toys, books, collectibles.

17   Iron Horse Antiques
1055 32nd Street (M-40 South)
Allegan   MI 49055
616 673-2674 or 616 673-9417
May to Oct.: Fri. Sat. & Sun. 12 to 5
East side of the highway.
Antiques, collectibles, and used horse tack.

OTSEGO

18   Little Red School House
793 West M-89
Otsego   MI 49080
616 692-3833
Sat. & Sun. 12 to 5, or by appointment.
Closed Jan. to March.
2 miles west of Otsego, northeast corner M-89 & 108th
Avenue.
Antiques and collectibles.

19   Heritage Antique Mall
621 M-89 West
Otsego   MI 49078
616 694-4226
Tues. to Sat. 10 to 5, Sun. 1 to 5
North side of highway, west of town.
60 dealers, 8,000 square feet.
General line of antiques, including lot's of furniture.

20   Rustic Ranch
106th & M-89
Otsego MI 49078
616 694-9320

21   The Mercantile
506 West M-89
Otsego   MI 49078
616 692-3630
Costumes, some antiques.

22   Otsego Antiques Mall
114 West Allegan Street (M-89)
Otsego   MI 49078
616 694-6440
Tues. to Sat. 10 to 6, Sun. 1 to 5
Downtown, north side of street.
35 dealers.

23   Harry J's & Missy
123 West Allegan
Otsego   MI 49078
616 694-4318

PLAINWELL

24   Plainwell Antiques
220 South Main
Plainwell   MI 49080
616 685-9030

25   Granny's Nook & Cranny
151 North Main Street
Plainwell   MI 49080
616 685-4183
Proposed to open in 1999 in former variety store building.

26   Junk'n Stuff'n Things
633 East Miller Road, east of 8th
Plainwell   MI 49080
616 685-5755

DOOR

27   Back Door Antiques & Gifts
4219 18th Street, north of 142nd Avenue
Dorr MI 49323
616 681-9415

WAYLAND

28   Unique Outlet
739 South Main Street
Wayland   MI 49323
616 792-6021
Web site: www.classic-link.com

3.2 Barry County

© 1998 AAA - used by permission.

HICKORY CORNERS

1   Hickory Hollow Antiques
14560 South Kellogg School Road, at Hickory Road
Hickory Corners   MI 49060
616 671-4222

DOSTER

2   The Elevator
12911 South Doster Road, north of M-89
Doster   MI 49080
616 664-4676

DELTON

3   Aunt Ellen's Attic
117 South Grove Street (M-43), downtown
Delton MI 49046
616 623-8900

MIDDLEVILLE

4   Becky's Mainstreet
9414 Spring Creek Court
Middleville MI 49333
616 795-8800

HASTINGS

5   Daval's Used Furniture & Antiques
2020 Gun Lake Road (M-37/M-43 West)
Hastings   MI 49058
616 948-2463

6   Pages Book Store
108 East State Street
Hastings MI 49058
616 948-2341
Books, toys and a few antiques.

7   Hastings Antique Mall
142 East State Street
Hastings   MI 49058
616 948-9644
Tue. to Sat. 10 to 6, Sun. 12 to 5   Mon. by chance.
Downtown, south side of the street.
2,200 square feet of antiques. Spinners & weavers gallery on
the 2nd floor.

8   Carlton Center Antiques
2305 East Carlton Center Road (M-43 northeast)
Hastings   MI 49058
616 948-9618

NASHVILLE

9   Mar-Jay Collectibles
232 N. Main (M-66)
Nashville   MI 49058
616 945-5965

© 1998 AAA - used by permission.

G = Grand Ledge: 9 - 11

EATON RAPIDS

1   Miller's Crossing Art & Antiques
203 South Main Street, at Island Park entrance
Eaton Rapids MI 48827

2   The Basket Case Antiques 'n Stuff
217 South Main Street
Eaton Rapids MI 48827
517 663-6100

3   Lita's Antiques & Treasures
142 South Main Street
Eaton Rapids MI 48827
517 663-7373
Tues. to Fri. 11 to 6, Sat. 10 to 4
Downtown
Featuring the Armani Collections; also furniture, glassware,
and jewelry.

CHARLOTTE

4   The Scottish Thistle
127 South Cochran
Charlotte MI 48813
517 541-1491

5   Windwalker Antiques & Fine Art Gallery
125 South Cochran
Charlotte MI 48813
517 543-9933
Tues. to Fri. 10 to 5, Sat. 10 to 4, Sun. 12 to 5
Just down from the Old Court House.
"Unusual objects for the discerning collector."

POTTERVILLE

6   Main Street Estate Shop
200 West Main Street
Potterville   MI 48876
517 645-2909
Main Street is the northern-most street in town.

7   Ken's Antiques
112 West Main Street
Potterville   MI 48876
No telephone listed.

8   Elliott's Emporium
6976 Windsor Highway
Potterville MI 48876
517 645-4545; 800 864-5380
Mon. to Sat. 10 to 6, Sun. 12 to 6
I-96 Exit 98A (Lansing Road) three miles southwest, or I-69
Exit 70 one mile southwest.
The Old Windsor Schoolhouse.   McCoy, lodge look, antler art,
primitives, etc. Visa, Master Card, Discovery Cards accepted.

GRAND LEDGE

9   Bridge Street Church Antique Mall
200 North Bridge Street
Grand Ledge   MI 48837
517 627-8637
Wed. to Sat. 10 to 5; Sun. 12 to 5
Downtown, northeast of the river.
2 floors, antiques & collectibles.

10   The Cat's Meow
117 East Scott Street
Grand Ledge   MI 48837
517 622-2000
Mon. to Sat. 10 to 5:30
One block southwest of the light, then left off the parking lot.
Antique & collectible glassware, dishes, 20's & 30's pieces,
linens, jewelry, prints, etc.

11   Grace Antiques and Fine Art
312 South Bridge Street
Grand Ledge   MI 48837
517 622-1524
Mon. & Wed. to Sat. 10 to 7, Sun. 12 to 5
Downtown, next to Sun Theater.
Antiques, vintage furniture, art pottery, jewelry, old books,
bronze statues, mission oak, oil paintings, and watercolors.

Grace
Antiques
& Fine Art

Cathy & Greg
(517) 622-1524

312 S. Bridge St.
Grand Ledge, MI 48837

Mon 10-7 • Closed Tuesday • Wed-Sat 10-7 • Sun 12-7

© 1998 AAA - used by permission.

Districts Within Ingham County:
W: Western Ingham County
E: Eastern Ingham County

M = Mason: 3 - 6
L = Lansing: 10 - 21
W = Williamston: 27 - 33

A. Western Ingham County

LESLIE

1 Anns'tiques
4202 Meridian Road
Leslie   MI 49251
517 589-9225
Wed., Sat. & Sun. 10 to 5
West side of road between Kinneville &
Fitchburg Roads 4.5 mi. east of U.S. 127.
General line of antiques, including:
furniture, pottery, collectibles, glass.

2   Leslie Antique Mall
149 South Main Street
Leslie   MI 49251
517 589-9430

MASON

3   Heard It Thru The Grapevine
4504 West Columbia Road, between Holt and Mason
Mason   MI 48854
517 676-2110
Mostly crafts; only two booths of antiques.

4   Art & Shirley's Antiques
1825 South Aurelius Road
Mason   MI 48854
517 628-2065
Mon. to Sat. 11 to 5. If nobody is in the shop, knock on the
door of the house in back.
From Route 127: West on Barnes Road 4 miles , then north a
quarter mile on Aurelius.
From Holt: 7.5 miles south on Aurelius.
Caning, restoring, refinishing, and furniture in the rough.

5   Wood n' Glass Antiques
3154 Holt Road
Mason   MI 48854
517 694-0120
rwgreen@aol.com
By chance or appointment.
Quarter mile east of U.S. 127.
Victorian and Fenton Glass.

6   Mason Antiques District
208 Mason Street
Mason   MI 48854
517 676-9753
Web page: www.antiquedist.com
Every day 10 to 6
Two blocks east of Cedar Street, a mile east of U.S. 127.
Mason Antiques District has 10 shops and over 45 dealers.
The individual shops are as follows:

6.01   Mason Antiques Market
111 Mason Street
517 676-9753
Every day 10 to 6

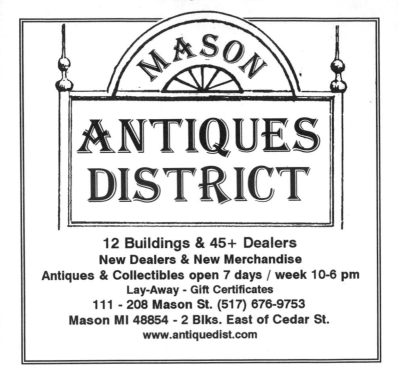

12 Buildings & 45+ Dealers
New Dealers & New Merchandise
Antiques & Collectibles open 7 days / week 10-6 pm
Lay-Away - Gift Certificates
111 - 208 Mason St. (517) 676-9753
Mason MI 48854 - 2 Blks. East of Cedar St.
www.antiquedist.com

6.02 Flamingo Road
111 Mason Street, upstairs from Mason Antiques Market
517 676-9753
7 Days 10 to 6;   Vintage apparel.

6.03 The Carriage Shop
208 Mason Street
517 676-1530
Wed. to Sun. 10 to 6   Toys, Dolls, Disney, Jewelry

6.04 Peddlar's Row
208 Mason Street
517 676-6388   Summer Only: Every Day 10 to 6
Outdoor sheds with rough to ready antiques & collectibles.

6.05 Front Porch Antiques Mall
208 Mason Street
517 676-6388
Every day 10 to 6   Advertising, antiques, collectibles.

6.06 The Loft Antiques Co-Op
208 Mason Street, upstairs from The Front Porch
517 676-0400   Wed. to Sun. 10 to 6
Country, Victorian, primitives, accessories.

SHOPS IN THE MASON ANTIQUES DISTRICT - continued

6.07   The Copper Kettle
Mason MI 48854
517 244-0414
Fri. & Sun. 12 to 5, Sat. 11 to 6
Southeast corner of the Mason Antiques District.

6.08   Old Mill Antiques Mall
207 Mason Street
517 676-1270
Every day 10 to 5
Furniture, glass, pottery, toys, advertising, coins, general line.

6.09   Rusty Nail Warehouse
208 Mason Street
Mason   MI 48854
517 676-1270
Every day 10 to 6;   furniture, collectibles, nostalgia, antiques.

6.10   The Secondary Market
208 Mason Street
Mason   MI 48854
517 676-6944   cookie jars, antiques and collectibles.

OKEMOS

7   Farm Village Antique Mall
3448 South Hagadorn Road
Okemos   MI 48864
517 337-4988;   Fax: 517 337-4560
Mon. to Sat. 11 to 6, Sun 12 to 6
Southeast corner Hagadorn & Jolly Road.
Large multi-level facility, over 50 dealers, 10,000 square feet.
Pottery, porcelain, furniture, books, jewelry, vintage clothing,
50's, Art Moderne and more.

8   Spud's Shop
3448 South Hagadorn Road
Okemos MI 48864
517 351-2140
Usually open Thurs. to Sun.
At Jolly and Hagadorn, just outside Farm Village Antique
Mall.
Exit I-96 at Okemos Exit, south to Jolly Road, 2 miles west to
Hagadorn.
Lamps, quilts, walking sticks, jewelry, eclectic good old stuff;
one of the most unique shops you will visit.

9   Wooden Skate Antiques, Estate Jewelry & Gems
1259 West Grand River Road
Okemos   MI 48864
517 349-1515;   FAX 517 349-8628;   E-mail:
sales@woodenskate.com
Web page: www.woodenskate.com
Mon. to Sat. 10 to 5:30, Thurs. to 8
Southwest corner Cornell Road & Grand River, 1.3 miles east
of Meridian Mall, 6 miles west of Williamston.
Large facility; huge estate jewelry department, Hummels,
China, furnishings, toys, silver, canes, clocks & watches, and
more.

LANSING

10   Antique Connection
5411 South Cedar Street
Lansing   MI 48911
517 882-8700
Mon. to Fri. 10 to 9; Sat. 10 to 6; Sun. 12 to 5
East side of street, in the rear of Furniture Connection furniture store, 1 mile north of I-96, 1 block south of Jolly Road.
Glass, smalls, books, antique furniture, some crafts, over 90
antique & collectibles booths.

11   Candlelight Antiques
3010 South Cedar
Lansing   MI 48911
517 887-6241
Wed. to Sat. 12 to 5;   closed Nov.
West side of street; parking in the rear.
General line of antiques.

12   St. Luke's Antiques
3016 South Cedar
Lansing MI 48910
517 882-5364

13   Somebody Else's Stuff
1137 South Washington
Lansing MI 48910
517 482-8886

14   Triola's Gallery
1114 East Mt. Hope Road
Lansing   MI 489120
517 484-5414
Deco and modernism design.

Map: City of Lansing:

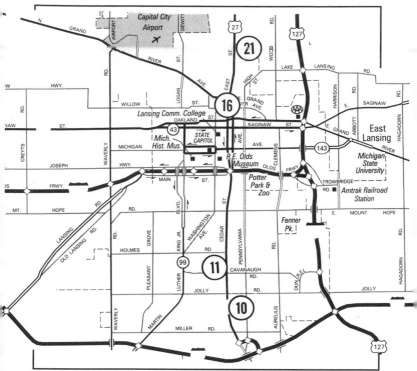

© 1998 AAA - used by permission.

15   Tom's Furniture & Antiques
319 East Grand River, west of Center Street
Lansing MI 48912
517 485-8335
Antiques, collectibles, new & used furniture.

16   Foibles
309 East Grand River Ave., between Washington and Cedar
Lansing MI 48910
517 485-5165

17   Trader Joe's
913 West Saginaw
Lansing MI 48912
517 374-5700

*Note: Bohnet's at 2918 North Grand River may have some
antique lighting fixtures.*

18   Pennyless in Paradise
1918 East Michigan, at Clemens
Lansing MI 48912
517 372-4526

19   Slightly Tarnished
2008 East Michigan
Lansing MI 48912
517 485-3599

20   The Little Red Schoolhouse
5002 West Saginaw (M-43), east of Lansing Mall
Lansing   MI 48917
517 321-6701   Mostly crafts, some antiques.

21   Mid Michigan Mega Mall
15487 U.S. Highway 27
Lansing MI 48906
517 487-3275
Daily 11 to 6, Thurs. to 8:30
North side of Lansing, two miles south of I-69.
Antiques, new furniture, unique gifts; over 200 dealers.

B. Ingham County, Eastern Portion

STOCKBRIDGE

22   Tom Forshee Antiques
119 West Main Street (rear)
Stockbridge   MI 49285
517 851-8114
Fri. & Sat. 10 to 4; Sun. 12 to 4; or by appointment.
South side of street. Entrance from the rear parking lot;
enter the parking lot from Wood Street southbound.   The
shop is at the red awning.
Oriental and English porcelains and American furniture.

23   White Oak Antiques
4665 East Cooper Road
Stockbridge   MI 49285
517 851-8151
7 days, By chance.
7 miles north of Stockbridge on M-52 (or 8 miles south of I-
96), and one-half mile east of M-52, on Cooper Road.
Antiques, china, glass, books, prints, furniture, plus paper and
collectible junk; 3 rooms stuffed full plus a barn.

24   Hafner Antique & Craft Mall
5000 South Clinton
Stockbridge MI 49285
517 851-7677

DANSVILLE

25   Rogers Antiques
1135 Mason Road (M-36 west)
Dansville   MI 48819
517 623-6566

26   Red Barn Antiques & Collectibles
1131 Mason Street (M-36 west)
Dansville   MI 48819
517 623-6631

WILLIAMSTON

27   Bittersweet Antiques
2200 Howell Road
Williamston MI 48895
517 655-1698
South 6 miles on Williamston, east on Howell Road.

28   Antiques Market of Williamston / Grand River
Merchants
2991 Williamston Road, north of I-96
Williamston   MI 48895
517 655-1350

29   Old Plank Road Antiques
126 West Grand River Avenue
Williamston   MI 48895
517 655-4273

30   Jolly Coachman
115 West Grand River
Williamston MI 48895
517 655-6606

31   Main Street Shoppe Antiques
108 West Grand River Avenue
Williamston   MI 48895
517 655-4005

32   Legends Jewelry
104 West Grand River Avenue
Williamston MI 48895
517 655-4221

33   Corner Cottage
120 High Street
Williamston   MI 48895
517 655-3257
Tues. to Sun 11 to 5
Downtown, one block north of traffic light, just east of
Putnam.
Specializing in quality oak furniture.

34   Tanglewood Antiques
102 South Putnam
Williamston   MI 48895
517 655-2128

35   Putnam Street Antiques
122 South Putnam Street, 2nd floor
Williamston   MI 48895
No telephone listed.

36   Lyons Den Antiques
132 South Putnam
Williamston   MI 48895
517 655-2622
Every Day 11 to 5, evenings by appointment.
Downtown, west side of the street, south of Grand River Ave.
"Quality antiques at affordable prices."

37   Canterbury Antiques
150 South Putnam Street
Williamston   MI 48895
517 655-6518

38   Things Beer
100 East Grand River Avenue
Williamston MI 48895
517 655-6701
Website: http://nervecore.com/thingsbeer/
Beer collectibles pre-prohibition to present.

39   Old Village Antiques
125 East Grand River Avenue
Williamston   MI 48895
517 655-4827
Wallace Nutting prints; Victorian furniture, art glass, etc.

40   Happicats Antiques
133 East Grand River Avenue
Williamston   MI 48895
517 655-1251; 517 223-8039
Cat collectibles, vintage clothing, old books, and antiques.

41   Sign of the Pineapple Antiques
137 East Grand River
Williamston   MI 48895
517 655-1905

42   House of Trivia
138 East Grand River Avenue
Williamston MI 48895
517 655-5570
Antique toys & trains.

43   The Rectory
326 East Grand River
Williamston MI 48895
517 655-6268
Parking in rear.

WEBBERVILLE

44   Iron Horses
4412 Grand River Road East (West side of town.)
Webberville MI 48892
517 521-4200

45   Re-Use It Antiques, Consignments & Collectibles
120 West Grand River
Webberville MI 48892
517 521-4390
Antiques & used furniture

ANTIQUES ON AMERICA ON LINE

If you are an AOL subscriber, type in the keyword ANTIQUES and
you will get a menu with the following choices: 1. A recent article
(e.g. "Antique Shopping on the Net" from the Nov. 12 1998 New
York Times); 2. AOL Classifieds - Antiques; and 3. An announce-
ment about a once-a-week (9 pm Sun.) Antiques Chat. Also included is a link to the E-bay auction site.

3.5 Livingston County

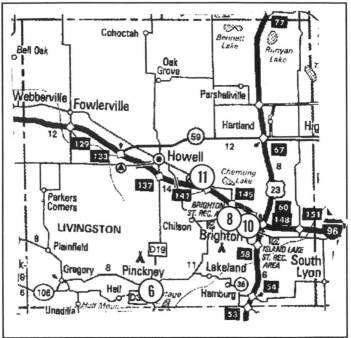

FOWLERVILLE

1   Ruth's Resale Shop
102 East Grand River Road
Fowlerville MI 48836
517 223-7221
Seldom open; Sat. by chance.

2   S & J Track Shack
514 South Grand Avenue
Fowlerville MI 48836
517 223-7442
I-96 Exit 129 north; west side of street at the tracks.

HOWELL

3   Antiques on the Avenue
315 North Michigan Avenue
Howell MI 48843
517 552-1080

4   Indian Hills Antiques
9480 Wiggins Road
Howell MI 48843
517 546-8792
Painted country furniture, reproduction lighting, etc.

5   Lake Chemung Oldies
5225 East Grand River Road, west of Chilson Road
Howell MI 48843
517 546-8875

PINCKNEY

6   Bloomers Antiques & Collectibles
545 East Main Street (M-36)
Pinckney MI 48169
734 878-8957
Tues. to Sun. 11 to 5
One block east of D-19 on M-36 (Main Street).
Charming turn-of-the-century Victorian house showcasing an
eclectic blend of antiques, collectibles, and primitives.

HARTLAND

7   Stillmeadow Shop
3568 Hartland Road
Hartland MI 48029
810 632-5560
Country gifts and antiques.

BRIGHTON

8   Nostalgia
116 West Main Street
Brighton MI 48116
810 229-4710;   E-mail: see2@webtv.net
Mon. to Wed. 10 to 7; Thurs. & Fri. 10 to 8; Sat. 10 to 6;
Sun. 12 to 5 by chance or appointment.
Downtown Brighton.
Furniture and a general line of antiques & collectibles.
New this year: Petite cafe with imported coffees & espresso;
1800's theme.

9   Entre' Nous Antiques and Accessories
323 West Main Street
Brighton MI 48116
810 229-8720
Household accessories, floral arrangements, and antiques.

10   The Quaker Shoppe Antiques
210 Hyne Street
Brighton MI 48116
810 229-6558
Thurs. to Sat. 11 to 4, or by appointment.
One block south of West Main Street, west side of street at
North Street.
Antiques, folkart, oil paintings, herb bouquets and wreaths.

11   History Town Antique Mall
6080 Grand River Avenue
Brighton MI 48114
517 545-9225
Tues. to Fri. 11 to 7, Sat. 10 to 4
From I-96 Exit 145 go west 3.2 miles on Grand River Avenue;
big white house on the hill between Howell & Brighton.
Victorian country & primitive furniture, cast iron, toys, lamps,
collectibles, etc.   Outdoor flea markets and auctions April to
October.   Ample front door parking.   Credit cards accepted.

12   Stock Exchange Antique Shop
1156 Hacker Road
Brighton MI 48114
810 227-7912   Open April through Oct.

HAMBURG

13   The Hamburg Store
10596 Hamburg Road, south of M-36
Hamburg MI 48139
810 231-6940
Michigan farmhouse antiques.

3.6 Oakland County

© 1998 AAA - used by permission.

R = Royal Oak: 9 - 37
B = Birmingham: 41 - 53
P = Pontiac: 54 - 58
H = Holly: 72 - 80

WALLED LAKE

1   Countryside Craft Mall & Antiques
1154 East West Maple Road, between Pontiac Trail & Decker
Walled Lake MI 48390
248 926-8650

FARMINGTON

2   Craftique Craft & Antique Mall
33300 Slocum, east of Farmington Road
Farmington MI 48336
248 471-7933
Web Site: www.craftique.com

SOUTHFIELD

3   The McDonnell House
19860 West 12 Mile Road
Southfield MI 48076
248 559-9120
Wed. to Sat.: 10 to 5, or by chance or appointment.
Just east of Evergreen, north side of road.
Antiques and collectibles.

FRANKLIN

4   D & J Bittker, Ltd.
26111 West 14 Mile Road, Suite 102
Franklin MI 48025
248 932-2660
Antique Chinese furniture, screens, textiles, and contemporary
Japanese ceramics.

BERKLEY

5   Timeless Antiques
2733 Woodward
Berkley MI 48072
248 582-1510

6   Twice Around Resale Shop
2966 West 12 Mile Road
Berkley MI 48072
248 545-6600
Tues. through Sat. 11 to 4
Downtown Berkley, north side of the street, next to Rite Aid
Pharmacy, same block as Berkley Theatre.
Antiques, collectibles, vintage jewelry.

7   Circa
3117 West Twelve Mile Road, between College & Greenfield
Berkley MI 48072
248 586-1930
Antiques, decorative items, etc.

FERNDALE

8   Sally Wright Antiques
22446 Woodward, south of Nine Mile Road
Ferndale MI 48220
248 399-0339
Old and reproduction lamps.

ROYAL OAK

9 Heritage Company II Architectural Artifacts & Design
Boutique also at this location: A Rose is a Rose
116 East 7th Street
Royal Oak MI 48067
248 547-0670
Mon. to Sat. 11 to 5
South of downtown just east of Main Street.
Architectural material, antiques, collectibles, & custom
architectural fabrication.
A Rose is a Rose boutique has china, linens, etc.

10   Del Giudice Gallery
515 South Lafayette Street, at 6th
Royal Oak MI 48067
248 399-2608

11   Milieu
308 West Fourth Street
Royal Oak MI 48067
248 542-9119

12   The Dandelion Shop
114 West Fourth Street, between Center & Main
Royal Oak MI 48067
248 547-6288

13   Deco Doug
106 West Fourth Street
Royal Oak MI 48067
248 547-3330
Mon. to Sat. 12 to 6
Downtown, North side of street.
Art Deco accessories, vintage watches, clocks, lamps.

14   The Cherub's Chest and **In The 20th Century**
112 East 4th Street
Royal Oak MI 48067
248 542-9594
Mon. to Sat. 10 to 6, Sun. 11 to 5; open to 5:30 in the winter.
South side of the street, one building east of Main Street.

The Cherub's Chest has a unique blend of French, nouveau,
deco, Trompe L O'eil, linens, lace, and more.

In the 20th Century has art deco, furniture, vintage clothing,
and textiles.

Map: Royal Oak Area:

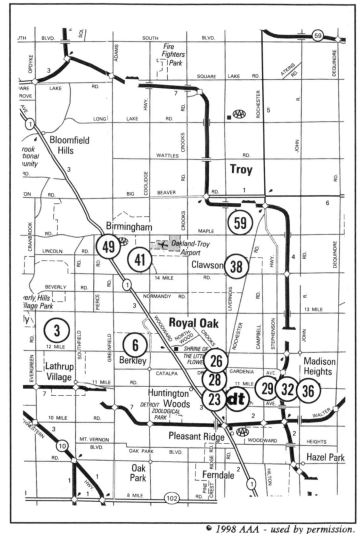

dt = Downtown Royal Oak: 10 - 22

15   Golden Girls Antiques
(May have a new name in 1999.)
324 East 4th Street
Royal Oak MI 48067
248 548-6350

16   Simpley Charming Antiques
325 East Fourth Street
Royal Oak MI 48067
248 541-9840

17   Jeffrey's 4th Street Antique Mall

404 East 4th Street
Royal Oak MI 48067
248 584-2220
Tues. to Sat. 11 to 7, Thurs. to 9; Sun. 12 to 5, Mon. by
appointment.
Largest collection of vintage American art pottery in the state.
Arts & crafts furniture.

18   Grandma's Good-Stuff
405 East Fourth Street
Royal Oak MI 48067
248 543-2335

19   Red Ribbon Antiques
418 East 4th Street
Royal Oak MI 48067
248 541-8117

20   Vertu Deco and Fifties
511 South Washington
Royal Oak MI 48067   248 545-6050

21   Carol Grant Decorative Arts

510 S. Washington
Royal Oak MI 48967
248 398-1311; Fax: 248 586-1104
Tues. to Sat. 11 to 5
West side of the street.
Arts & crafts furniture and pottery; primitive painted
furniture; antique garden accessories.

22   Daves Comics & Collectibles
407 South Washington
Royal Oak MI 48067   248 548-1230

23 Yellow House Antiques

125 North Washington
Royal Oak MI 48067
248 541-2866
Mon. to Sat. 11 to 5, Sun. 12 to 5
West side of street, north of 11 Mile Road.
Primitives, Fifties, decorative accessories, Victorian, and a
general line.

24   The Coach House of Metamora
429 N. Washington
Royal Oak   MI 48067
248 547-2640

25   Vertu II
433 North Washington
Royal Oak   MI 48067
248 547-3062

26   House on Main
803 North Main Street
Royal Oak   MI 48067

248 544-7358;
Fax: 248 398-5033

Mon. to Sat. 12 to 4,
closed Tues.

North of downtown,
west side of the street
at Austin Street
between 11 and
11 1/2 Mile Roads,
across from the
Hollywood Market.

Pottery, vintage
photographs, silver,
glass, textiles etc.

A shop in the rear
does vintage cards,
stationery, and
invitations.

House On Main

Judith Weiner

803 N. Main
Royal Oak
Michigan 48067
Ph: 248 ·544·7358
Fx: 248 ·398·5033

27   Antiques on Main
115 South Main Street
Royal Oak   MI 48067
248 545-4663

28   Lulu
405 North Main Street
Royal Oak   MI 48067
248 542-6464
Mon. thru Sat. 11 to 5.
Downtown, west side of street, 2 blocks north of 11 Mile Road.
Buttons, primitives, ceramics, and eclectic.

29   Jeff Fontana Designs
500 West Eleven Mile Road
Royal Oak MI 48067
248 543-8370
Mon. to Fri. 11:30 to 5, Sat. 12 to 4
2 blocks west of Washington.
Design studio & European antiques & accessories.

30   Royal Oak Farmers Market
316 East 11 Mile Road, 2 miles east of Woodward
Royal Oak MI 48067
248 548-8822
Sunday 8:30 to 4; some antique dealers open during the week
as well.
The Farmers Market is owned by the City of Royal Oak.

31   Cantrell Antiques & Collectibles
600 East 11 Mile Road
Royal Oak MI 48067
248 398-0646

32   Antique Connection
710 East Eleven Mile Road
Royal Oak MI 48067
248 542-5042; Fax: 248 542-3660
www.quikpage.com/a/antiqueconn
Tues. to Sun. 10 to 5
South side of the road.

33   White Elephant Antique Shop
724 West Eleven Mile Road, east of Woodward
Royal Oak MI 48067
248 543-5140

34   Antiques Unlimited
831 East 11 Mile Road
Royal Oak MI 48067
248 545-4488

35   Royal Antiques
1106 East Eleven Mile Road
Royal Oak MI 48067
248 548-5230

36   Lovejoy's Antiques
720 East Eleven Mile Road
Royal Oak MI 48067
248 545-9060;   Fax: 284 545-8641
E-mail: luvjoy720@aol.com
Tues. to Sun. 10 to 5, Fri. 12 to 5
South side of the road.
General line, specializing in reverse painted lamps.

37   Craftique Craft & Antique Mall
30947 Woodward Avenue, at 13 Mile Road
Royal Oak MI 48073
248 288-4400

CLAWSON

38   Aquilon Antiques
26 North Main
Clawson MI 48017
248 577-5255
Web sites: www.acquilon.com
                    www.bigbook.com/aquilon
Tues. to Sat. 11 to 6
Downtown, just north of 14 Mile Road, east side of the street.
Glassware, jewelry, furniture, gold & silver, etc.

MADISON HEIGHTS

39   Ben Wulff Antiques
918 West 11 Mile Road, just east of the expressway
Madison Heights MI 48071
248 545-4488
Lighting, etc.

COMMERCE

40   Byers Country Store
213 Commerce Road, west of Carol Lake Road
Commerce MI 48382
248 363-3638

BIRMINGHAM

41   Classic Country Antiques
2277 Cole
Birmingham MI 48009
248 258-5140
Mon. to Fri. 11 to 5, Sat. 12 to 4
In a warehouse district between 14 Mile & 15 Mile Road, east
of Woodward, just east of Eton.
American & English antique furniture and accessories.

42   James Sanders, Antiquarian
725 South Adams Road
Birmingham MI 48009
248 540-0044
In the South Adams Square Building, east side of street.

43   Chase Antiques
251 East Merrill Street, second floor
Birmingham Mi 48009
248 433-1810; 810 543-4511
Merrillwood Building, 1 block south of Maple.

44   Crimson Rose Antiques
251 East Merrill Street, second floor
Birmingham MI
248 203-2950

45   The Cowboy Trader Gallery
251 East Merrill Street, second floor
Birmingham MI 48009
248 647-8833
Second floor.
Small shop; western art and a few antiques.

46   Leonard Berry Antiques
251 East Merrill Street, second floor
Birmingham MI 48009
248 646-1996

47   Troy Corners Antiques in Birmingham
251 East Merrill Street, second floor
Birmingham MI 48009
248 594-8330

48   L'Esprit
243 West Maple
Birmingham MI 48009
248 646-8822

49   Watch Hill Antiques
330 East Maple
Birmingham MI 48009
248 644-7445; Fax: 248 644-1152
www.watchhillantiques.com
Mon. to Sat. 10 to 6, Thurs. & Fri. to 8; Sun. 12 to 4
South side of street between Woodward and Old Woodward.
Country antiques and accessories from Europe, specializing in
original painted furniture, pine TV centers, pine tables, chairs
and mirrors.

50   CeCe's
335 East Maple
Birmingham MI 48009
248 647-1069; Fax: 248 647-3005
Art and antiques.

51   O' Susannah
570 North Old Woodward Avenue
Birmingham MI 48009
248 642-4250
Architectural artifacts, country primitives, gifts, etc.

52   Merwins Antique Gallery
588 North Old Woodward, just south of public parking lot.
Birmingham MI 48009
248 258-3211

53   Madeline's Antique Shoppe
790 North Old Woodward, north of Vinewood
Birmingham MI 48011
248 644-2493

PONTIAC

54   Scott Emporium
196 & 198 West Walton Blvd.
Pontiac MI 49770
248 338-4148

55   Modern Age
25 North Saginaw Street
Pontiac MI 49770
248 745-0999; 888 861-8479; Fax: 248 745-9598
E-Mail: kzuc@aol.com
Wed. to Sat. 12 to 6
5,000 sq. ft. on 3 levels; 20th Century design & decorative arts.
"Finest selection of 20th Century decorative arts in Michigan."

56   First 1/2
43 North Saginaw Street
Pontiac MI 49770
248-334-9660; Fax: 248 253-1883
jcaussin@aol.com
www.machineage.com
Wed. to Sat. 12 to 6
Downtown, west side of the street.
20th Century design; furniture, lighting objects, etc.

57   The Antique Gallery
102 North Saginaw Street
Pontiac MI 49770
248 334-1154

Note: A map of the Pontiac area appears on the following page.

Map: City of Pontiac:

© 1998 AAA - used by permission.

58   Dixieland Antique Flea Market
2045 Dixie Highway, at Telegraph Road
Pontiac MI 49770
248 338-3220
Fri., Sat. & Sun.

TROY

59   Judy Frankel & Associates
2900 West Maple Road, Suite 111
Troy   MI 48040
248 649-4399
judy@judyfrankelantiques.com
Mon. to Wed. 10 to 4, Thurs. 10 to 12, or by appointment.
Lower level of Somerset Plaza office building, next to
Somerset Plaza shopping center, northeast corner Maple &
Cooledge.
Antiques and decorative arts.

(See Display Ad on opposite page.)

ROCHESTER HILLS

60 Hidden Treasures
2155 West Auburn
Rochester Hills MI 48069
248 299-9555

ROCHESTER

61 Antiques by Pamela
319 Main Street
Rochester MI 48063
248 652-0866; Fax: 248 652-0866
E-Mail: pjk@speedlink.net
Mon. to Fri. 10 to 6, Sat. 10 to 5, Thurs. to 8
Use Main Street or back parking lot entrances.
Graduate gemologist on staff.   Contemporary, vintage and
antique jewelry.   Victorian through Retro period in
furniture, crystal, lighting, sterling; many accessories.

62 Haig Galleries
311 Main Street, Floor Two
Rochester MI 48063
248 656-8333;   Ancient, Asian, Tribal antique art.

63 Chapman House on Main
329 Main Street
Rochester MI 48063
248 651-2157

64   Tally Ho! Antiques
404 Main Street
Rochester MI 48063
248 652-6860
Mon. to Fri. 12 to 6, Sat. 10 to 5, Thurs. to 8
Use Main Street or back parking lot entrances.
Period antiquities in furniture, jewelry, crystal, clocks, books,
primitives, sterling and more.

65   Haig Jewelers
436 South Main
Rochester MI 48063
248 652-3660

WATERFORD

66   The Great Midwestern Antique Emporium
5233 Dixie Highway (U.S. 24), south of Andersonville Road
Waterford MI 48329
248 623-7460;   50 dealers, 5,500 square feet

67   Shoppe Of Antiquity
7766 Highland (M-59), east of Williams Lake Road
Waterford MI 48329
248 666-2333

68   Ann's 5th Avenue Antique Shop
2045 Dixie Highway, at Telegraph Road
Waterford MI 48329
248 745-1915

CLARKSTON

69   The Parsonage
6 East Church Street
Clarkston MI 48346
248 625-4340
Mon. to Fri. 9 to 6, Sat. 9 to 5
I-75 Exit 91 to Downtown Clarkston.
Flowers, gifts, and antique furniture.

70   Clarkston Country Store / Main Street Antiques
21 North Main
Clarkston MI 48346
248 625-3122

71   Pour Mary's Antiques & Things
5878 Dixie Highway, north of Andersonville Road
Clarkston MI 48346
248 623-3250

HOLLY

72   Battle Alley Arcade
108 Battle Alley, next to Holly Hotel
Holly   MI 48442
248 634-8800

73   Angora Antiques
110 Battle Alley, lower level of Holly Hotel.
Holly   MI 48442
248 634-0000

74   Home Sweet Home Antiques
101 South Saginaw Street
Holly MI 48442
248 634-3925

75   Beverley's Two
114 South Saginaw Street
Holly MI 48442
248 634-5974   Gifts, flowers, linens, bears, crafts, antiques.

76   Holly Antiques on Main
118 South Saginaw Street
Holly   MI 48442
248 634-7696

77   Cottage Antiques
203 South Saginaw Street
Holly MI 48422
248 328-0018

78   Balcony Row Antiques
216 South Broad Street
Holly MI 48442
248 634-1400

79   Holly Crossing Antiques
219 South Broad Street
Holly MI 48442   248 634-3333

80   Water Tower Antiques Mall
310 South Broad Street
Holly MI 48442   248 634-3500

ORTONVILLE

81   The Stone House
850 Ortonville Road (M-15), 8 miles north of I-75
Ortonville MI 48462   248 627-5380

OXFORD

82   Sunset Antiques Inc.
22 North Washington Street
Oxford MI 48371   248-628-1111

83   Past Times Antiques
27 West Burdick
Oxford MI 48371
248 628-9939
Thurs. to Sat. 10 to 6
Downtown, just off M-24.
General line of antiques.

84   Oxford Antique Mall
18 North Washington Street (M-24)
Oxford MI 48371
248 969-1951; Fax: 248 969-0376
Every day 11 to 6, Thurs. to Sat. Until 9
Downtown, east side of the street.
6,500 square feet of quality antiques. Dolls, primitives, clocks,
china, pottery, fine furniture, weather vanes, juke boxes, etc.

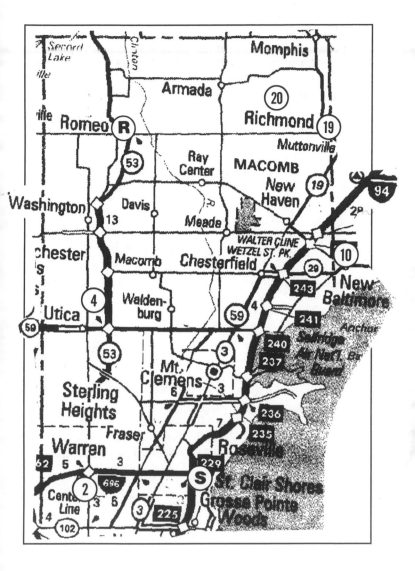

WARREN

1   Fred's Antique Furniture & Antiques
14091 8 Mile Road, west of Gratiot
Warren MI 48089
810 776-7100

1.5 Antique Gallery
11564 13 Mile Road
Warren   MI 48089   810 751-0063

2   Silver Quill Antiques

22813 Van Dyke
Warren MI 48089
810 756-8180
Mon. Tues. Fri. & Sat. 12 to 6, Sun. 1 to 6
Two blocks south of Nine Mile Road, northwest corner Maxwell Street.
Glass, china, pottery, jewelry, etc.

━━━ STERLING HEIGHTS ━━━

3   Countryside Craft Mall & Antiques
40700 Van Dyke Avenue, at 18 Mile Road
Sterling Heights MI 48313   810 977-1633

3.5 Moravian Trail Shop
34355 Moravian Trail
Sterling Heights MI 48313   810 979-4101

━━━ UTICA ━━━

4   Bear Lair

2100 Auburn Rd.
Utica MI 48317
810 731-2894
Mon. to Sat. 10 to 5; Sun. 12 to 4
North a half mile from M-59 on Dequindre, next to the Hollywood Market.
General line, specializing in paper items & advertising.

━━━ ST. CLAIR SHORES ━━━

5   Adams English Antiques

19717 Nine Mile Road
St. Clair Shores MI 48080
810 777-1652
Mon. to Fri. 9 to 5, Sat. 10 to 5
Six blocks west of Harper, just east of I-94, north side of road.
Custom harvest tables, wardrobes, and scrub pine specialty.

6   Attic Crafts & Antiques

24518 Harper
St. Clair Shores MI 48081
810 776-4790
Tues. to Sat. 10 to 6, Sun. 12 to 5
4 blocks south of 10 Mile Road.
25+ dealers. Dolls, primitives, trunks, crafts, glassware, China, furniture, jewelry, pottery, toys, advertising, doll repair, etc.

7   McHugh's Antiques
23215 Nine Mack Loop
St. Clair Shores MI 48080
810 774-9966

8   Toodles
26717 Little Mack, south of 11 Mile Road
St. Clair Shores MI 48081
810 772-0920
In Victoria Place House of Shoppes.

MT. CLEMENS

9   Estate Antiques & Resale
1142 Southbound Gratiot Ave.
Mount Clemens MI 48043
810 468-9888

NEW BALTIMORE

10   Heritage Square Antique Mall
36821 Green Street (M-29)
New Baltimore MI 48047
810 725-2453
Tues. to Sat. 10 to 5; Sun 11 to 5
Northeast of downtown on M-29 past the light, north side of
street in a large white 1861 mansion.
20 dealers; wide variety of quality antiques.

11   Washington Street Station
51059 Washington Street
New Baltimore   MI 48047
810 716-8810

WASHINGTON

12   Bank of Antiques
58415 Van Dyke (M-53), north of 26 Mile Road
Washington MI 48094
810 781-5647; 810 798-3283

ROMEO

13   Carriage Trade Antiques
264 North Main
Romeo MI 48065
810 752-7778

14   Sherry's Antiquery
222 North Main
Romeo MI 48041
810 752-9860

15   Romeo Antique Mall
218 North Main Street
Romeo MI 48065
810 752-6440

16   Town Hall Antiques
205 North Main
Romeo MI 48065
810 752-5422
Daily 10 to 6
Downtown, west side of street just north of the light at 32
Mile Road.
50 dealers; quality antiques.

17   A Matter of Taste
105 South Main
Romeo MI 48065
810 752-5652

18   Remember When Antiques & Collectibles
143 West St. Clair (32 Mile Road)
Romeo MI 48307
810 752-5499
Tues., Wed., Thurs. & Sat. 10:30 to 5:30; Sun. 12 to 4
White house 2 blocks west of Main, (old Van Dyke) south
side of street.
A general line, specializing in glassware, pottery and china of
the Depression Era; also furniture; thousands of Wades.

RICHMOND

19   Barb's Antique Mall
69394 Main Street (M-19)
Richmond MI 48062
810 727-2826
Tues. to Sun. 12 to 5
North end of downtown, 3 blocks north of Division Street,
east side of street.
Antiques, Depression Glass, oak & Victorian furniture.

20   High Bank Antiques
28689 Armada Ridge Road
Richmond MI 48062
810 784-5302
Fri. to Sun. 12 to 5, Tues. by chance or appointment.
From Richmond: At the north end of downtown go west on
Park Street; this becomes Armada Ridge Road.   Continue
out of town several miles.   The shop is on the north side of
the road, midway between Richmond and Armada.
250 antique lighting fixtures; furniture, and miscellaneous.

21   Lou Capp
68286 South Main Street (M-19), south of downtown
Richmond MI 48041
No telephone.
Large building of used furniture, collectibles, and antiques.

22   Wagon Wheel Antiques
69273 Main Street
Richmond MI 48062
810 727-7474

MEMPHIS

23   Sherry's Antiquery
80515 South Main Street (M 19)
Memphis MI 48041
810 392-2989

ARMADA

24   Parkway Antiques
23046 Main Street
Armada MI 48002
810 784-5682
Downtown, south side of street.

Map: City of Holland:

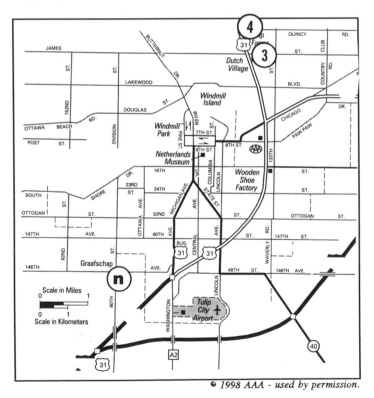

© 1998 AAA - used by permission.

n = Nob Hill, located in Allegan County; see page 92

TIER 4:
GRAND RAPIDS-FLINT-
PORT HURON

4.1 Ottawa County

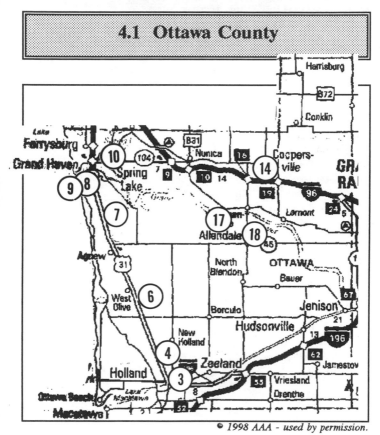

© *1998 AAA - used by permission.*

HOLLAND

One shop with a Holland address is located in Allegan County.

1   The Brick House
112 Waukazoo Drive
Holland   MI 49423
616 399-9690

2   Twigs
185 South River Avenue
Holland   MI 49423
616 392-2775
Consignment items; a few antiques.

3   Harvest Antiques & Collectibles
Horizon Outlet Center
12330 James Street
Holland MI 49424
616 395-0823
Mon. to Sat. 10 to 8, Sun. 10 to 6
The Harvest Outlet Center is at U.S. 31 & James Street.
Harvest Antiques & Collectibles is located between Eddie
Bauer & Bugle Boy at the east end of the mall.
Hummel, furniture, NASCAR, advertising, World Fair goods,
glassware, miniatures, etc.

4   Tulip City Antique Mall
3500 U.S. 31
Holland   MI 49424
616 786-4424; Fax: 616 786-4426;
Web Site: www.classic-link.com/tulipcity.htm
Mon. to Sat. 10 to 6; Sun. 12 to 6
Corner of Greenly, east side of the highway, 2 miles north of
M-21 interchange.
30,000 square feet, 200 dealers.   Dolls, glass, fine china,
pottery, radios, Indian artifacts, vintage clothing, etc.

Tulip City Antique Mall

200 Dealers
30,000 square feet
of
Quality Antiques
and Collectibles

3500 U.S. 31
(Corner of Greenly & 31)
Holland, MI 49424
(616) 786-4424
Fax (616) 786-4426

WEST OLIVE

5   Whispering Pines Antiques
6427 Butternut Drive
West Olive   MI 49460
616 399-6216

6   Lake Shore
Antique Shop

10300 West Olive
Road (U.S. 31)

West Olive
MI 49460

616 847-2429
Fax:
616 847-7101

March-Dec.:
Mon.-Sat. 10-6;
Sun. 12-5
Jan. & Feb:
Mon.-Sat. 10-5;
Sun. 12-5

7 mi. south of
Grand Haven,
east side of
highway.

Quality antiques
& collectibles,
glass, pottery,
quilts, furniture.

Lake Shore Antiques

**10300 West Olive Road
West Olive MI
616 847-2429**
Buy & sell antiques.   Estate Sales
Open 7 days a week except special holidays.

GRAND HAVEN

7   **West Michigan Antique Mall**
13279 168th Street at U.S. 31 South
Grand Haven   MI 49417
616 842-0370
E-mail: Leavittsq@novagate.com
Mon. to Sat. 10 to 6; Sun. 12 to 6
On U.S. 31 at Ferris, 2 miles south of Grand Haven.
12,000 square feet.

8   Whims and Wishes
216 Washington
Grand Haven   MI 49417
616 842-9533
Mon. to Thurs. 10 to 6, Fri. 19 to 8, Sat. 10 to 5
South side of Washington west of U.S. 31.
Antique jewelry & silver; furniture, glassware, and
contemporary gifts.

9   Carriage House Antiques
122 Franklin Avenue
Grand Haven MI 49417
616 844-0580
Tues. to Sat. 11 to 5; Sun. 1 to 5;   Closed Jan. and Feb.
One block south of Washington between 1st and 2nd Streets,
entrance and parking in rear.
2 floors of Victorian and country furniture & accessories, glass,
crystal, silver, copper, linen, estate jewelry. Expert assistance.

SPRING LAKE

10   Spring Lake Antique Mall
801 West Savidge (M-104)
Spring Lake   MI 49456
616 846-1774
Summer: Mon. to Sat. 10 to 6; Sun. 12 to 5;
Winter: Mon. to Sat. 10 to 5, Sun. 12 to 5
North side of road, just east of the Spring Lake bridge.
50 dealers, 4,400 square feet. Glassware, primitives, furniture,
collectibles, North Woods, Chitz China, jewelry, marbles, etc.

COOPERSVILLE

11   Coopersville Antiques & Collectibles
6862 Arthur Road West, I-96 Exit 16
Coopersville MI 49404
616 837-8547

12   Ye Olde Post Office
286 Ottawa Street
Coopersville   MI 49404
616 837-9475;   Gifts, country crafts, antiques.

13   Main Street Antiques
265 Main Street
Coopersville MI 49404
616 837-1937
Main Street is one-way east-bound.

14   The Re-Find Shop
244 West Randall
Coopersville   MI 49404
616 837-5814
Mon. to Fri. 10 to 6, Sat. 10 to 5
Downtown
Antiques, collectibles, housewares, used furniture.
"An estate Sale in a Showroom."

15   Mostly Antiques
16694 48th Avenue, north of I-69 Exit 19
Coopersville   MI 49404
616 837-9695

LAMONT

16   Maple Valley Antiques
13575 42nd Avenue, at Johnson
Lamont
616 677-3422;   Country, primitives.

ALLENDALE

17   Antiques of Allendale
6821 Lake Michigan Drive (Highway M-45)
Allendale MI 49401
616 892-6022
Mon. to Sat. 9:30 to 5:30; Sun. 12 to 5
Two doors west of the light, north side of the street.
Approximately 40 dealers.   E-bay name: woz

18   Ward's Antiques
5187 Lake Michigan Drive (M-45)
Allendale   MI 49401
616-895-7015
Thurs. Fri. & Sat. 10 to 5, or by appointment.
North side of road, west of Grand Valley State University.
2 floors of quality furniture, advertising, toys, glassware, etc.

ART DECO ON THE INTERNET

An internet gateway to art deco design and antiques is:

www.deco-echoes.com

Another art deco website is www.machineage.com which deals with
20th Century design.   Included is a dealer directory, an on-line
store, classified ads, and a directory of art deco organizations
throughout the country.

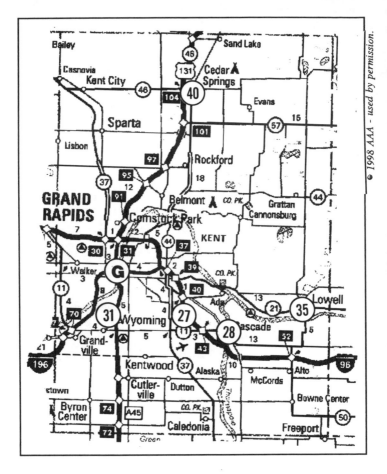

© 1998 AAA - used by permission.

G = Grand Rapids: 1 - 29

GRAND RAPIDS

1 Plaza Antique Mall
1410 28th Street SE
Grand Rapids   MI 49506
616 243-2465
Mon. to Fri. 10 to 7; Sat. 10 to 6; Sun. 1 to 5.
South side of the highway, a block west of Kalamazoo Road.
68 dealers, 9,000 square feet. Air conditioned; Visa & Master
Card Accepted.
Oak furniture, lamps, glassware, china, pottery, etc.

(See Display Ad on opposite page.)

2   Marlene's Antiques & Collectibles
1054 West Fulton,
Grand Rapids MI 49504,   616 235-1336

3   Treasures
442 West Leonard
Grand Rapids   MI 49504
616 742-0360
Mon. to Sat. 10 to 6
One and a half blocks west of U.S. 131.
Antiques, stamps, coins, jewelry, Collectibles.

4   Reflections Antiques
532 Leonard St. NW
Grand Rapids   MI 49504
616-458-0388;   E-mail: antiques@iserv.net
Mon. to Fri. 10:30 to 6:30, Sun. 10 to 5
4 blocks west of U.S. 131
20 dealers, 7,500 square feet.   1950's furniture, sterling, china,
jewelry, toys, garden items, Victorian, and shabby chic.

5   Mary's Used Furnishings
730 Leonard NW
Grand Rapids   MI 49504
616 774-8792
Mon. to Sat. 10 to 6
1.5 miles west of Highway 131, just past Arnie's Restaurant, at
McReynolds Street.
Antiques, accessories, and used furniture.

6   One Man's Junk
450 Leonard, east of Highway 131
Grand Rapids   MI 49504   616 456-9100

Map of Grand Rapids:

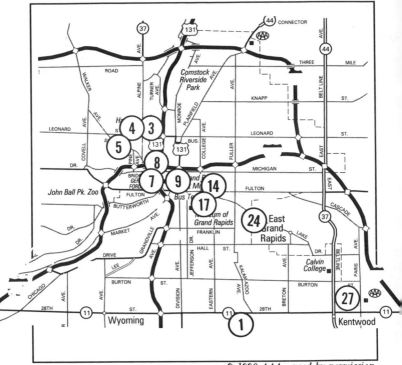

7   The Green Man Antiques
444 Bridge Street NW
Grand Rapids   MI 49504
616 454-5771
Wed. to Sun. 11:30 to 5:30;
Oct. to June: closed between 3 & 4 weekdays.
South side of the street, across from Antiques by the Bridge.
Furniture and a general line of antiques.

8   Antiques by the Bridge
445 Bridge N.W.
Grand Rapids   MI 49504
616 451-3430
Tue. to Sat. 10 to 5; Sun. 12 to 5
North side of street, just west of Broadway, across the river
from downtown.
Note: Bridge Street becomes Michigan Street east of the river.
20 dealers, 9,500 square feet, 3 floors.

One of the dealers, Mayfield Antiques, specializes in mission
oak furniture & arts & crafts period decorative objects.

9   Curiosity Shop
220 Lyon Street NW   Suite 215
Grand Rapids   MI 49503
616 454-7879
Mon. to Sat. 10:30 to 5:30
Suite 215 of the Amway Grand Plaza Hotel.
Smalls, China, books.

10   A Scavenger Hunt II: Antiques & Classics
2 Jefferson SE., at Fulton
Grand Rapids   MI 49501
616 454-9955 or 800 344-4868
20th Century Designer Moderne furniture & decorative items.

11   A Scavenger Hunt
210 E. Fulton
Grand Rapids   MI 49503
616 454-1033
1930's to 50's designer furniture; vintage clothing.

12   Collage: A World of Buttons
940 Monroe
Grand Rapids   MI 49504
616 451-2572

13   Nobody's Sweetheart
953 East Fulton
Grand Rapids   MI 49503
616 454-1673
Antiques, vintage clothing, jewelry, accessories, antique lamps,
pottery, textiles. Religious collectibles, kitchen collectibles,

14   East Fulton Antique Mall
959 East Fulton Street
Grand Rapids   MI 49503
616 774-3320
Tues. to Sat. 11 to 6
One mile east of downtown Grand Rapids, near Diamond
Street, next to Van's Pastry Shop.

15   Lighthouse Furnishings
1317 East Fulton
Grand Rapids   MI 49503
616 458-8212

16   Cherry Hill Market
721 Cherry Street SE
Grand Rapids   MI 49508
616 776-0266   Antiques and grocery items.

17   Bygones
910 Cherry Street
Grand Rapids   MI 49508
616 336-8447
Tues. to Fri. 11 to 5, Sat. 10 to 5, Sun. 11 to 3
Heritage Hill area.
General line, plus primitives.

18   Heartwood
956 Cherry Street SE, at Warren
Grand Rapids   MI 49506
616 454-1478
Mission; Art Deco; and other 20th Century decorative arts.

19   Phil's Stuff
724 Wealthy Street SE, at Charles
Grand Rapids   MI 49503
616 455-1940

20   Acauthus Antiques
1035 Wealthy Street SE
Grand Rapids   MI 49503
616 235-3467

21   Wealthy Street Antiques
1052 Wealthy Street SE
Grand Rapids   MI 49503
616 774-2776

22   Cobblestone Antiques
1440 Wealthy Street SE
Grand Rapids   MI 49503
616 774-3483   1950's furniture, etc.

23   Wood Wizards
1500 Wealthy Street SE
Grand Rapids   MI 49503
616 458-5448

24   Theadora's
2166 Wealthy Street
East Grand Rapids MI 49506
616 458-4755
Pager: 616 562-8707
Call for hours.
Between Croswell & Bagley, Gaslight Village area.
"A wonderful place to discover."   Antiques, estate furnishings,
& quality consignments.   "Buy and sell."
(See Display Ad on opposite page.)

25 Turn of the Century Antiques
7337 South Division
Grand Rapids   MI 49508
616 455-2060
Adjacent to Grand Rapids Furniture.   Music boxes.

26 Koning's Wood Products
7226 South Division
Grand Rapids   MI 49508
616 455-1780

27 The Antique Gallery, Inc.
3545 28th Street SE; Eastbrook Mall
Grand Rapids   MI 49512
616 977-0981; Fax: 616 977-0985
Mon. through Sat. 10 to 9; Sun. 12 to 5
In the southwest wing of the shopping center.
Coins, jewelry, china, furniture, magazines, post cards, toys, trains, etc.

28 Yarrington Antiques
6718 Old 28th Street SE
Grand Rapids   MI 49546
616-956-6800
Tues. to Fri. 11 to 5; Sat. 10 to 5, other times by chance.
Take 28th Street 1.7 miles from the I-96 / 28th Street junction. Turn right onto Old 28th Street.
"A delightful blend of odd and unusual, quaint and beautiful Art Glass, Porcelains, Glassware, Pottery, Furniture, Jewelry, Lighting, Paper Items, Tools, Country Antiques, etc. A quality shop with treasures arriving daily."

29   Home Sweet Home
2717 Kraft SE, east of I-96
Grand Rapids   MI 49512
616 949-7788
Antiques & gifts.

WYOMING

30   Village Antiques & Lighting
1334 Burton SW, east of Burling Game, south of Lee.
Wyoming MI 49518
616 452-6975

31   Pack Rat Antique Mall
4907 S. Division
Wyoming MI 49518
616 249-0588; Fax: 616 249-0780
E-mail: packratco@aol.com
Mon. to Fri. 12 to 7, Sat. 10 to 6
West side of highway.
Antiques, collectibles, furniture, gifts.

GRANDVILLE

32   Memories Antique Mall
3125 28th Street SW Suite A, east of I-196
Grandville MI 49418
616 538-1010

33   Sheri's Antiques
3948 30th Street Suite A
Grandville   MI 49418
16 249-8066

34   The Grainary Antique Shop
44th Street - Rivertown Parkway
Grandville MI 49418
616 534-6651

LOWELL

35   Cranberry Urn Antiques
208 East Main
Lowell   MI 49331
616 897-9890; (616 897-9145 res.)
Tue. Wed. Fri. & Sat. 11 to 5
South side of street, east end of downtown; pull into the
parking lot just east of the bridge.
Glass lamp shades, dolls, and a general line of antiques.

36   Flat River Antique Mall
212 West Main Street
Lowell   MI 49331
616 897-5360
40,000 square feet, 5 floors.

37   Main Street Antique Mall
221 West Main Street
Lowell   MI 49331
616 897-5521

ROCKFORD

38   Rockford Antique Mall
54 Courtland
Rockford   MI 49341
616 866-8240   Web site: www.rockfordantique.com

39   Time Travelers
480 Northland Drive, at 11 Mile Road
Rockford   MI 49341
616 866-9368

CEDAR SPRINGS

40   Red Flannel Antique Co.
128 North Main Street
Cedar Springs   MI 49319
616 696-9599
Tues. to Fri. 11 to 4, Sat. & Sun. by chance or appointment.
Downtown on Old U.S. 131, east side of street.
Pine, primitives & general line; large book department.

41   Mercantile of Yesterday
17 North Main Street
Cedar Springs   MI 49319
616 696-9945

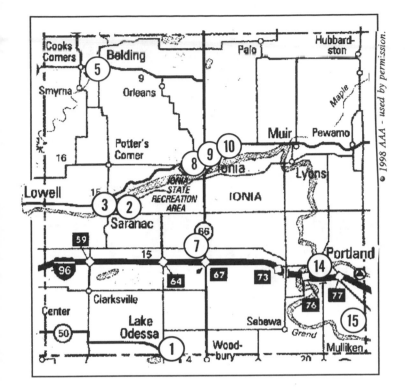

© 1998 AAA - used by permission.

LAKE ODESSA

1 Lake-O Downtown Mall Antiques & Collectibles
1012 4th Avenue
Lake Odessa MI 48849
616 374-3089
Wed. 10 to 8, Sat. 10 to 5, Sun. 10 to 5
On M-50, off I-96, off M-66.

SARANAC

2 Saranac Antique Exchange
28 Vosper
Saranac   MI 48881
616 642-6291
www.theantiquexchange.com

April to Dec.: Wed. to Sat. 10 to 6, Sun. 1 to 5;
Jan. to March.: Sat. 10 to 6, Sun. 1 to 5
2 blocks east of downtown in a vintage school building.
Multi dealer shop; general line. Also: auction facility.

3   Pine Ridge Antiques & Collectibles
75 Bridge Street
Saranac   MI 48881
616 642-0362
Wed. to Sat. 11 to 5;   closed Dec. 25 through Jan. 1
Located downtown, west side of the street, in an 1880's
building approximately 1/2 mile south M-21.
General line of antiques including furniture, glassware &
pottery. Visa/Mastercard accepted.
Additional parking a block west.

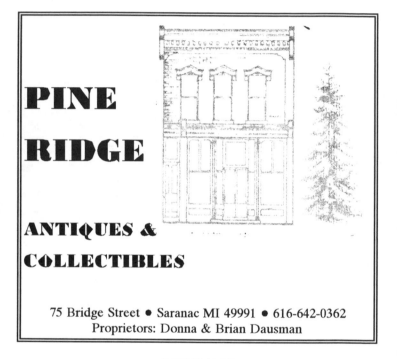

PINE
RIDGE

ANTIQUES &
COLLECTIBLES

75 Bridge Street ● Saranac MI 49991 ● 616-642-0362
Proprietors: Donna & Brian Dausman

ORLEANS

4   Village Antique Shoppe
5517 Orleans Road South
Orleans   MI 48865   616 761-3888

BELDING

5   Mari-Mar Sales
1439 W State (M-44)
Belding   MI 48809
616 794-2423
Mon. to Wed. and Fri. & Sat. 10 to 5
Red barn set back from road; south side of M-44 between
Bridge St. & M-91.
Furniture; glassware; dolls; jewelry and collectibles.

6   Countryside Floral Gifts & Antique Shop
224 West State (M-44)
Belding   MI 48809
616 794-0921 or 1-800 842-3137

IONIA

7   Grand River Antiques
7050 South State
Ionia   MI 48846
616 527-8880
Every Day 10 to 5
M-66 a quarter mile north of I-96 Exit 67, west side of
highway.
Thirty dealers; everything from primitives to Victorian;
outstanding inventory of vintage clothing; Indian artifacts;
excellent furniture, etc.
"The coffee is always on."

8   Fire Barn Antiques
219 West Washington Street
Ionia MI 48446
616 527-2240
Wed. to Sat. 10 to 5, Fri. to 6; Sun. 12 to 5
South side of street, next to Post Office, 1 block off Main
Street -- in an old fire station.
General line of antiques.

FIRE BARN ANTIQUES
Chris & Beth Woodard
P R O P R I E T O R S
219 West Washington Street
IONIA, MI 48846
[616] 527-2240

9   Ionia Antique Mall
415 West Main
Ionia   MI 48846
616 527-6720
Mon. to Sat.: 10 to 5, Fri. to 8, Sun. 12 to 5
Downtown, south side of the street a half block from M-66.
One dealer specializes in fishing lures and all forms of
hunting & fishing collectibles, tools, and men's stuff.

10   Keynote
316 West Main Street
Ionia   MI 48846
616 527-2262
Wed. to Sun. 11 to 5
Downtown north side of the street.
Player pianos; general line.

11   Checkerboard Antiques
524 West Lincoln Ave.
Ionia MI 48846
616 527-1785;   E-mail: checkers@iserv.net

12   Past Time
764 West David Highway
Ionia MI 48846
616 527-4587

PORTLAND

13   McMillen & Wife Antiques
9073 South State Road
Portland   MI 48875;   616 374-8088

14   Two Peas in a Pod
170 Kent Street
Portland   MI 48910
517 647-6577
Tues. to Sat. 11:30 to 6
Downtown, east side of the street.
Antiques and fine art.

15   McMillen & Husband
11464 McCrumb Road
Portland   MI 48875
517 627-2794
Sat. & Sun. 10 to 5, weekdays by chance or appointment.
From Portland: east on Grand River to Clintonia, go south to
the second road, go right one half mile.
Art glass, pottery, Beanie Babies, etc.

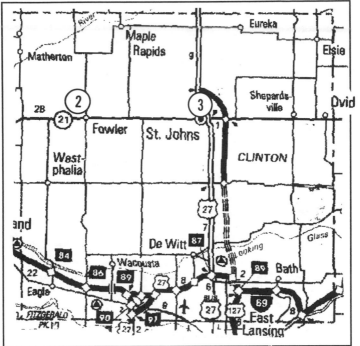

© 1998 AAA - used by permission.

DeWITT

1   Liberty Antique Mall
1161 East Clark Road, #310 Lansing Factory Outlet Stores
DeWitt MI 48820
517 669-4050
20,000 square feet.

FOWLER

2   Savannah's Secret Garden
108 Main St.
Fowler MI 48835
517 593-3012
Wed. to Fri. 10 to 7, Sat. 10 to 5,
Sun. 12 to 5
A block north of M-21 from the light,
west side of the street.
Gifts, crafts, antiques.

153

ST. JOHNS

3   Antiques & Friends
115 Clinton Avenue North
Saint Johns MI 48879
517 224-4473
Mon. to Thurs. 10 to 6, Sat. 10 to 5, Sun. 12 to 5
Downtown, west side of street, half block north of Square.

4   Irrer Antiques
201 West McConnell
St. Johns MI 48879
517 224-4085
White house, southwest corner Church & McConnell Streets;

5   Antiques & Collectibles
601 West Cass Street
St. Johns MI 48879
517 224-3864

6   Jerry Nickel Antiques
1300 N. Lansing Street
St. Johns MI 48879
517 224-6248
Bibles, books, gifts, music, antiques.

7   County Line Antiques
2021 South County Line Rd
St. Johns MI 48879
517 224-6285
Northeast corner U.S. 27 & County Line Road, 8 miles north.

8   Barnside Antiques
1991 County Line Road, at U.S. 27
St. Johns MI 48879
517 224-8212

OVID & ELSIE

9   Parkers Furniture
108 North Main Street
Ovid MI 48866
517 834-2287;   Some antiques.

10   Melvin Antiques & Clock Shop
8401 Island Road (West Main Street)
Elsie MI 48831
517 862-4322

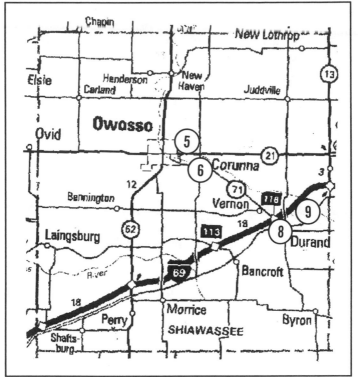

© 1998 AAA - used by permission.

PERRY

1   Bobbie's Gifts & Collectibles
10980 South M-52, south of I-69
Perry MI 48872
517 625-7817

OWOSSO

2   Studio 415
415 West Main Street
Owosso MI 48867
517 729-6018

3   Curiosity Shop
113 North Washington
Owosso MI 48867
517 725-1589

155

4   Midtown Antiques Mall
1426 North M-52
Owosso MI 48867
517 723-8604

5   "I REMEMBER THAT"
2085 East Main Street
Owosso MI 48867
517 723-9397
Mon. to Sat. 10 to 5, closed Wed. & Sun.
Located on M-21 east of Owosso, halfway between Walmart
and Meijer on north side of the street.
Look for bright pink sign.
12 dealers; glass, furniture, pottery, kitch.

CORUNNA

6   Ken's Consignment Resale Shop
231 North Shiawassee (M-71)
Corunna MI 48817
517 743-3329;   517 743-5744   E-mail: kenndot@shianet.org
Thursday 10 to 5, Fri. 10 to 8, Sat. 10 to 5
At the "Main Corner" in downtown Corunna, at the light,
across from the Court House.
General line of antiques, collectibles and usables.

DURAND

7   Collectors Knot
218 West Main Street
Durand MI 48449
810 621-4014

8   Our Place
122 North Saginaw
Durand MI 48429
517 288-5856
Mon. to Sat. 10 to 6, Sun. 11 to 5
Downtown.
Antiques & crafts.

9   The Country Cupboard
10260 East Bennington Road
Durand MI 48429
517 288-3659
April to Dec.: Thurs. to Sat. 10 to 5
Three miles northeast of town, between Brown and New
Lothrup Roads.
General line, primitives, country, & hand spinning fleeces,
roving and battings.

THE COMPLETE ANTIQUE SHOP DIRECTORY INTERNET SITE:

www.AntiqueShops.net

Starting in March, 1999 the Internet web site for Complete
Antique Shop Directories should be operational.   This web
site will contain a listing of those Michigan antique shops that
contributed to the cost of printing this book and maintaining
the web site.

Through this site you will be kept informed of new shops that
open within the state, as well as shops listed in this book that
may close during the year.   There will also be a more com-
prehensive listing of antique shows than is possible in this
book.   (See page 187 for the listing of selected Michigan
antiques shows.)   Also included in the www.AntiqueShops.net
web site will be links to other internet sites of interest to
Michigan antique dealers and collectors.

Dealers opening new shops (or closing them) should fax
information about their shop to 616 469-0455 in order to be
added to the web site and to the next edition of this book.

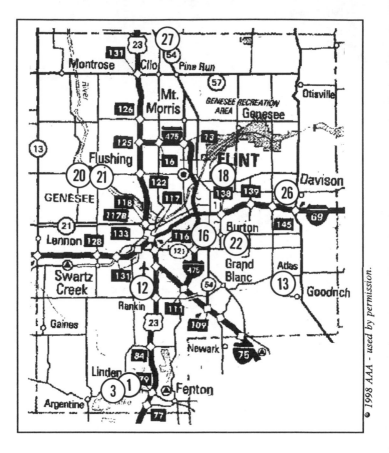

© 1998 AAA - used by permission.

LINDEN

1   Thimbleberry Antiques
101 North Bridge Street
Linden MI 48451
810 735-7324
Tues. to Sat. 11 to 5; Sun. 12 to 5; Fri. & Sat. evenings on
occasion.
Downtown at the light, three miles west of U.S. 23, Silver
Lake Road exit.
Antiques, art glass, gifts, furniture, lamps, and Old World
Christmas.

2   The Tangled Vine Antiques & Gifts
109 North Bridge Street
Linden MI 48451
810 735-4611

3   Susan's Woven Seats
116 West Broad Street
Linden MI 48451
810 735-5854, 810 735-5832
Wed. 10 to 4; Thurs. and Fri. 2 to 4; Sat. 10 to 12
North side of street, 2nd floor above a teddy bear shop.
Caning supplies of all kinds. Antiques, specializing in
hammered aluminum.

4   This & That Shop Antiques & Things
416 West Broad Street
Linden MI 48451
810 735-4234

5   North Side Antiques
918 North Bridge Street
Linden MI 48451
810 735-7752

FENTON

6   The Iron Grate
103 West Shiawassee Avenue
Fenton MI 48430
810 629-3434
Decorative accessories, a few antiques.

7   The Gathering
115 Mill, at Adelaide
Fenton MI 48430
810 750-0877

8   The Incurable Collector
208 North Bridge
Fenton MI 48430
810 735-1067

9   Fenton Bean Company
234 North Leroy
Fenton MI 48430
810 750-4595

10   McGehee's Closet
300 South Leroy
Fenton   MI 48430
810 750-8008
Custom made lamp shades and supplies; very few antiques.

11   Stuff 'N Such
11440 Torrey Road, south of Thompson
Fenton MI 48430
810 629-4613

SWARTZ CREEK

12   Memories Antique Mall
4036 West Grand Blanc Road
Swartz Creek (Rankin) MI 48473
810 655-8306
Tues. to Sat. 12 to 6, Sun. 12 to 5
North side of the road, a mile west of U.S. 23.
General line of antiques, and select accessories for the home.
Over 50 dealers.

ATLAS

13   Maurice Reid Antiques
8470 Perry Road
Atlas MI 48411
810 636-2414
Open April through Nov. by chance or appointment.
Five miles east of Grand Blanc to the village of Atlas.
Specializing in quality American Furniture from the Federal
period.

FLINT

14   Countryside Crafts Mall & Antiques
4333 Miller Road
Flint MI 48507
810 230-0885

15   Rebel's Junque
4442 Torrey Road
Flint MI 48507
810 238-0882
2 blocks north of Maple Street; South of Bishop Airport.

16   Reminisce Antique Gallery
3124 South Dort Highway
Flint MI 48507
810 744-1090
Daily 10 to 6, Sun. 12 to 6
I-69 Dort Highway Exit, south three traffic lights; just north of
Atherton.
Attractive mall with "good old stuff".

Map of Flint:

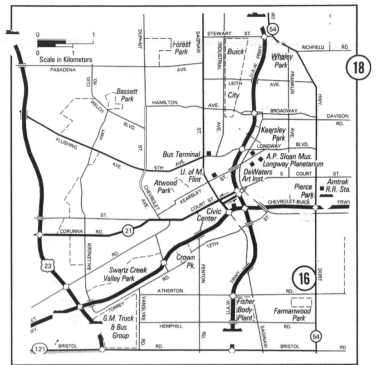

© 1998 AAA - used by permission.

17   Flint Public Flea Market
2411 North Franklin Street
Flint MI 48507
810 238-1862
Six blocks north of Davison; parking off Belle Avenue.

18   Antiques By Cecilia
G-3106 North Center Road
Flint MI 48506
810 736-0800
Mon. to Fri. 11 to 7, Sat. 11 to 5
In strip mall east side of Center Road, 1/2 block south of
Richfield.
Glass, porcelain, lamps, dolls, and general line.

FLUSHING

19   Timeless Memories
110 East Main Street
Flushing MI 48433
810 659-8622

20   Trudy's Antiques & N. Dean Mosey Jr. Woodworks
113 North McKinley Road
Flushing MI 48433
810 659-9801
Tues. to Sat. 10:30 to 5
East end of Downtown, half block north of Main St., west side of the street.
General line of antiques; custom refinishing, and custom designed furniture & accessories.

21   R & J Needful Things Antique Center, Inc.
6398 West Pierson Road
Flushing MI 48433
810 659-2663
www.antiqueit.com
Seven Days 10 to 5
North side of street, 2 1/2 miles west of I-75, Exit 122.
170 dealers.

BURTON

22   My Country Home
4067 East Court Street
Burton   MI 48509
810 742-6570 \ 810-742-0433
Mon. to Fri. 11 to 5:30, Sat. 11 to 4
Midway down a small strip mall, north side of the highway, across from Courtland Center.   Next to Art Van Furniture.
Antique primitives, antique cupboards, and country crafts.

Important Note: Don't let Junior the cat out when you enter or leave the shop.

23   Esquire
3140 East Atherton Road
Burton MI 48509
810 742-4968
Between Dort Highway & Center Road.

DAVISON

24   Village Square Antiques
305 North State (M-15)
Davison MI 48423
810 653-2835

25   Victorian Treasures
923 North State (M-15)
Davison MI 48423
810 658-3709
Two miles north of I-69.

26   Small Town Coins & Collectibles
7498 East Davison Road
Davison MI 48423
810 658-1992
www.concentric.net/towncoin
Mon. to Fri. 10 to 5, Sat. 10 to 3
In small mall, one mile north of I-69, southwest corner Irish & Dacison Roads.
Coins, antique toys, pedal cars & Pez.

CLIO

27   Brothers and Sisters
14100 North Saginaw (M-54)
Clio MI 48420
810 687-1294
Mon. to Sat. 10 to 6, Sun. 1 to 5
2.5 miles north of M-57, 3 miles south of Birch Run.
General line.

28   Marie's Barn Antiques
G-12213 North Saginaw (M-83)
Clio MI 48420
810 687-5270

29   Matthew's Antiques
G 12180 North Saginaw
Clio MI 48420
810 686-5148

Mt. MORRIS

30   Antique Mall America
I-75 & Mt. Morris Road, I-75 Exit 126
Mt. Morris MI 48458
810 564-1056

31   Attic Memories
G 9394 North Saginaw
Mt. Morris MI 48458
810 687-4804

4.7 Lapeer County

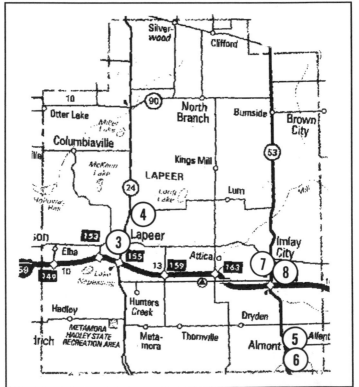

© *1998 AAA - used by permission.*

COLUMBIAVILLE

1   Christina's Antiques & Things
5155 Stanley Road
Columbiaville MI 48421
810 793-2762

LAPEER

2   Twice Is Nice Classics, Inc.
477 West Nepessing
Lapeer MI 48446
810 664-8463

3   Kingsmill Antiques
340 West Nepessing
Lapeer MI 48446
810 245-0971
Mon. to Wed. & Fri. & Sat. 10 to 6, Thurs. 12 to 5
Downtown, north side of the street.
Mission furniture, general antiques and Indian artifacts.

Kingsmill Antiques
& Collectibles

We buy and sell antiques and Indian artifacts

Ray and Glynis Kitchen, Owners

340 W. Nepessing St.   **(810) 245-0971**
Lapeer, MI 48446   (810) 667-1212 Fax

4   Past Tense Antiques
1965 Farnsworth Road
Lapeer   MI 48446
810 664-5559
Mon. to Sat. 10 to 6; Sun. 12 to 6
Two and a half miles north of Lapeer. Just south of Daley
Road, west side of the road.
Gifts, crafts, candles, antiques, silk floral and year-round
Christmas shop. Also: a cider mill.

ALMONT

5   Second Time Around
122 South Main Street
Almont MI 48003
810 798-2454
5 a.m. to 10 p.m.
Downtown, west
Antiques, collectibles, furniture, glassware, etc; also a coffee shop.

6   Stoney River Mercantile Antiques at the Shops of King's Mill
622 South Main Street
Almont MI 48003
810 798-8214
Tue. to Fri. 10 to 4, Sat. 10 to 5, Sun. 12 to 4
In historic King's Mill building.

IMLAY CITY

7   Monarch Monograms & Antiques
143 N. Almont Ave.
Imlay City MI 48444
810 724-3447
E-mail: jherman63@aol.com
Tues. to Fri. 9:30 to 5, Sat. 10 to 3; Sun. 12 to 4
M-53 north to 4th Street, west 3 blocks, left on Almont Ave., first block.   West side of the street.

8   Memory Junction
244 East Third Street
Imlay City MI 48444
810 724-4811;   Fax: 810 724-6590
E-mail: antiques@cardina.net
Mon. to Sat. 10 to 5, Sun. by chance.
Exit 168 from I-69, north on M-53 1.5 miles, then one block west on Third Street.
General line, Staffordshire, furniture, pattern glassware, Depression Glass, etc.

9   Re-Sale Shop
7567 Imlay City Road (Old M-21), east of M-53
Imlay City MI 48444
810 724-1082
Collectibles, used stuff, etc. In business since 1948.

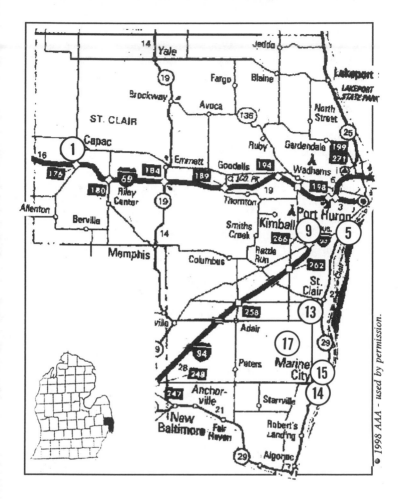

© 1998 AAA - used by permission.

CAPAC
---

1   Yesterday's Shadows
107 North Main Street
Capac MI 48014
810 395-4100
Tue. & Thurs. 12 to 5; Wed. & Fri. 10 to 7; Sat. 10 to 5, Sun.
1 to 5
Downtown, west side of street.
Antiques, crafts, and collectibles. Space for rent,
consignments accepted.

Are you interested in owning an antique shop? Call Sandy
Ulman about buying Yesterday's Shadows.

2   Treasures in the Rough
126 North Main Street
Capac MI 48014
No telephone listed.
Crafts, collectibles, country whimsy, some antiques.

LAKEPORT

3   Antique Workshop
7077 Lakeshore (M-25)
Lakeport MI 48059
810 385-4344

PORT HURON

4   The Wooden Spool
2513 10th Avenue, at Church Street
Port Huron MI 48060
810 982-3390
Country items, furniture, oil lamps, antiques.

5   Colonial Used Furniture Outlet
1219 Military Street
Port Huron MI 48060
810 987-4001
Mon. to Fri. 10 to 5:30, Sat. 10 to 5, Sun. 12 to 4
South of downtown; west side of street between Court and
Union.
Used furniture, antiques and collectibles.

6   Antique Collectors Corner
1603 Griswold Street
Port Huron MI 48060
810 982-2780
Griswold is Business Route I-69 west-bound.

7   Yesterday's Treasures
4490 Lapeer Road West, at Range Road
Port Huron MI 48060
810 982-2100
Antiques, coins, stamps, gifts, collectibles.

8   Ron's Place
2600 N. Range Road
Port Huron MI 48060
810 966-7965
Just in back of Yesterday's Treasures.

Map: City of Port Huron:

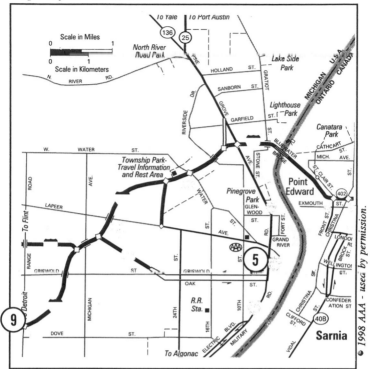

© 1998 AAA - used by permission.

KIMBALL

9   Artisans Antiques Collectibles Crafts
1661 Range Road Ste B-200
Kimball MI 48074
810 364-1255
Mon. to Sat. 10 to 9, Sun. 11 to 6
Northwest corner I-94 Exit 269 and Range Road.
In the far western end of the Horizon Outlet Mall.
16,000 square feet.   Furniture and a general line of antiques.

ST. CLAIR

10   Rivertown Antiques
201 North Riverside, Riverview Plaza Shopping Center
St. Clair   MI 48079
810 329-1020   May be closing in 1999.

11   Jennifer's Trunk
201 North Riverside, Riverview Plaza Shopping Center
St. Clair MI 48079
810 329-2032   Art and folk art.

12   Antique Inn
302 Thornapple, at Third Street
St. Clair MI 48079
810 329-5833

13   John Moffett Antiques
1102 South 7th Street
St. Clair MI 48079
810 329-3300
Wed. to Sun 12 to 5
From M-29: at the south end of downtown go north on
Clinton, then south on F.W. Moore Highway.   Red brick
building north of the Highway.
General line of antiques: junk to good stuff.

MARINE CITY

14   Marine City Antique Warehouse
105 Fairbanks (M-29)
Marine City MI 48039
810 765-1119
Mon. to Sat. 10 to 5, Sun. 12 to 5
In Bell River Plaza just west of the bridge, south side of the
highway.
Two floors of the largest selection of fine antiques and
collectibles in the Tri-County area.

15   Old Times N Such
213 Broadway Street
Marine City MI 48039
810 765-9577
Thurs. to Sat. 12 to 5, Sun. by chance.
Downtown, south side of the street.

16   The Snuggery
8540 North River Road (MI Route 29)
Marine City MI 48039
810 765-4737

CHINA

17   Red Barn Antiques, Crafts & Collectibles
4950 King Road
China   MI 48054
810 765-9453
Fri. to Mon. 10 to 4
King Road is a mile west of downtown Marine City; north on
King Road to just past Meisner Road; west side of road.

TIER 5:
THE M-46 ROUTE

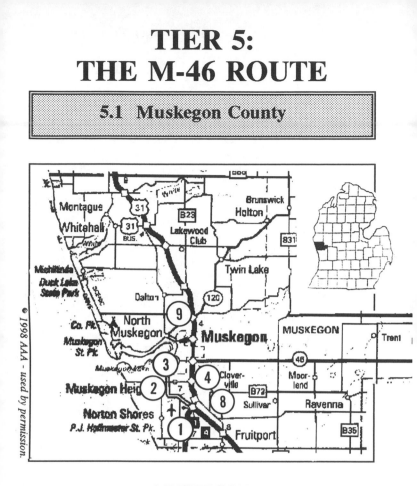

© 1998 AAA - used by permission.

MUSKEGON

1 Airport Antique Mall
4206 Grand Haven Road
Muskegon (Norton Shores) MI 49441
616 798-3318
Mon. to Sat. 11 to 6; Sun. 12 to 6
South from Muskegon on Business U.S. 31, exit on Grand
Haven Road; the mall is several blocks south at the southeast
corner of Airport Road.
Antiques & collectibles; mostly glassware & smalls.
25 dealers, 5,000 square feet.

2 Jewelry & Sundries
933 West Broadway
Muskegon MI 49441
616 759-1312
Tues. through Sat. 12 to 6
From Business U.S. 31 go west on Summit to Henry, north on
Henry to Broadway, west on Broadway a block and a half.
Military relics, Native American items, collectibles, jewelry.
Also silversmithing and lapidary supplies.

Map of Muskegon:

© 1998 AAA - used by permission.

3 Downtown Muskegon Antique Mall

1321 Division
Muskegon   MI 49441
616 728-0305
Mon. to Thurs. 10 to 5; Fri. & Sat. 10 to 7; Sunday 1 to 5
Lakeview Center, west of downtown, across from Muskegon
Lake.   From U.S. 31 go west on Laketon to Division, then
north.   Old Shaw Walker Building at Western & Division.
15,000 square feet.

Antiques &
Collectibles, plus
Handmade Accessories

Suite 10
1321 Division
Muskegon, MI 49441

(616) 728-0305

Bonnie Garrison

4   Mandy's Antiques
1950 East Laketon Avenue
Muskegon   MI 49441
616 777-1428
Mon. to Fri. 1 to 4; Sat. 10 to 3
2 blocks east of U.S. 31, Laketon Exit, north side of street at
Port City Road.
In business 25 years.

5   Station Antiques
2204 McCracken, at Milner
Muskegon   MI 49441
616 759-6708   Proposed to open early 1999.

6   Old Grange Mall
2783 Apple Avenue, at Walker Road
Muskegon MI 49442
616 773-5683
Set up like an old country store.

7   Strippers of Muskegon
3535 Getty, south of Sherman Street
Muskegon   MI 49441
616 733-2201 or 616 733-2824

CLOVERVILLE

8   Cloverville Mall
3165 Heights Ravenia Road
Cloverville MI 49442
616 773-5703
Tues. to Sat. 10:30 to 6, Sun. 12 to 5
From the south on I-96 go north on U.S. 31 two miles to
Sherman Blvd. (County B-72); go east two miles; road bends
and becomes Black Creek Road, then Heights Ravenna Road;
mall is at southeast corner Dangel Road.
Antiques, furniture, collectibles, crafts.

NORTH MUSKEGON

9   Memory Lane Antique Mall
2073 Holton Road
North Muskegon   MI 49445
616 744-8510
Mon. to Sat. 10 to 6, Sun. 11 to 4
Northwest corner M-120 & U.S. 31 Expressway.   Enter from
Roberts Road a block west of U.S. 31.
37 dealers, 6,000 square feet. Opened in 1992.

WHITEHALL

10   Pages & Friends Antique Shop
121 W. Colby
Whitehall   MI 49461   616 894-5980

11   From Time to Time Gallery
214 East Colby
Whitehall MI 49461   616 894-9569

12   Martha's Vineyard Antiques
4075 Lakewood Road, at Zeller
Whitehall   MI 49461   616 894-6602

BAILEY

13   The Tin Man
1414 Newaygo Road
Bailey   MI 49303
616 834-7141   E-mail: jctinman@webtv.net

ANTIQUE SHOP DIRECTORY ORDER FORM

_____   The Michigan Complete Antique Shop
          Directory $6.95

_____   The Alabama & Mississippi Complete Antique
          Shop Directory $6.95

_____   Taylor's Guide to Antique Shops in Illinois
          & Southern Wisconsin $4.95

_____   Iowa's Complete Guide to Antique Shops $4.95

Add $1.25 postage for one book, $1.75 for two books, $2.25
for Three or more books. Michigan residents add 6 percent
sales tax. Make checks payable to "Antique Shop Directories."

Name: _____

Address: _____

City, State, Zip: _____

Complete Antique Shop Directories
P.O. Box 297
Lakeside MI 49116

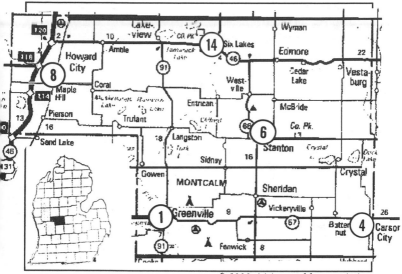

© 1998 AAA - used by permission.

GREENVILLE

1 Greenville Antique Center
404 South LaFayette Street
Greenville   MI 48838
616 754-5540
Sun. to Wed. 11 to 6, Thurs. Fri. & Sat. 11 to 8
Corner of M-57 & M-91, just south of downtown; loft building on east side of street.
5 floors, 35,000 square feet, 75 dealers.

2 Red Pump Antiques
West M-57, Victoria's Mercantile
Greenville   MI 48838
616 754-8991
Crystal, China, primitives, quality estate items.

CARSON CITY

3 Butternut Antique Shop
7948 South Street
Carson City   MI 48811
517 235-4398
3 miles west on M-57, north 1/4 mile on Crystal, west at the group of mailboxes.

4   Cook's Crossing
105 west Main Street
Carson City MI 48811
517 584-3677
Tues. to Fri. 11 to 5; Sat. 10 to 3
Downtown, south side of the street.
Three floors, 9,000 square feet.

STANTON

5   Grapevine Treasures
107 Main Street
Stanton MI 48888
517 831-8115   Antiques, vintage clothing, collectibles.

6   Hotel Montcalm
106 South Camburn
Stanton MI 48888
517 831-5055
Downtown, Main Street (M-66) & Camburn Street.
Unique Setting in historic hotel; reasonable prices.
Newly opened ice cream parlor and restaurant.

VESTABURG

7   Ora Deila Antiques
9881 Cannonsville
Vestaburg   MI 48891   517 268-5143

HOWARD CITY

8   Haack's Antiques
413 Muenscher
Howard City   MI 49329
616 937-4494
Always open. Knock on house door if shop is closed.
Old US 131 south from downtown two blocks to Chestnut,
west over the tracks on Chestnut to Muenscher, then south
two buildings.
Lots of furniture, old light fixtures, and reproduction china
cabinets.

AMBLE

9   Amble Antiques and Collectibles
14766 M-46, east of Amble Road
Amble   MI 49322
616 762-4548

LAKEVIEW

10   Tara II Antiques and Stuff
531 Lincoln
Lakeview   MI 48850
616 937-5148 Res.

11   Granny's Antiques
9535 Fitzner Road, at M-46
Lakeview   MI 48850
517 352-6030

12   Welcome Inn
7477 M-46, at Fitzner Street
Lakeview MI 48850
517 352-6393

SIX LAKES

13   Gambrel Gables
1014 Howard City Road
Six Lakes   MI 48886
517 427-5906

14   The Intersection
101 East Bridge Street
Six Lakes   MI 48886
517 365-3773; Fax: 517 365-3506;   E-mail: oovy@excite.com
Mon. to Sat. 10 to 8
3 blocks north of M-46, 3 blocks east of M-66, at Clark Street.
Antiques in the room to the left. Also: stained glass art studio -
residential & commercial commissions and restorations.

15   The Potato Been
3572 West Fleck Road
Six Lakes   MI 48886
517 365-3477

EDMORE

16   Moore's Antiques
406 East Main Street
Edmore MI 48829
517 427-3378

17   Country Charm
5167 East Howard City Road
Edmore MI 48829
Country crafts and some antiques.

5.3 Gratiot County

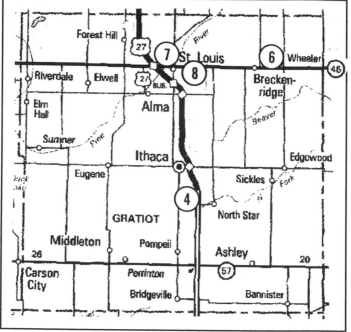

© 1998 AAA - used by permission.

ELWELL

1 Mac Lachlan House Antiques
6482 North Pingree Road, at Kates Drive
Elwell   MI 48832
517 463-1512
Vintage radio and phonograph items, etc.

ALMA

2 Unique Antiques & Gifts
2268 W. Monroe Road (M-46)
Alma MI 48801
A block east of U.S. 27, north side of M-46.

ITHACA

3 North Star Trader
3036 South Bagley Road, U.S. 27
Ithaca   MI 48847
517 875-4341 or 517 838-4409

4   Countryside Antiques
2024 South Bagley (U.S. 27)
Ithaca   MI 48847
517 875-2349
Mon. to Sat. 10 to 5, Sunday 1 to 6
West side of U.S. 27, north of Buchanan Road.
Full line of period lamp shades; old & new lamps; custom
built lamps from your artifacts; lamp repair.

WHEELER

5   Auntie Q's
8150 North Mason
Wheeler MI 48662
517 842-5862

BRECKENRIDGE

6   Hawkmur Antiques
Monroe Road (M-46)
Breckenridge   MI 48662
517 842-5456
Fri. to Sun. 10 to 5
East of U.S. 27 between Breckenridge & Wheeler, north side
of the highway.

ST. LOUIS

7   Tried and True Antique Mall
1694 West Monroe Road (M-46)
St. Louis MI 48880
517 681-2487
Mon. to Sat. 10 to 6, Sun. 12 to 5
One mile east of U.S. 27, north side of the highway.
Large variety of antiques and collectibles.

8   Middle of the Mitten
603 East Washington (M-46)
St. Louis MI 48880
Phone & Fax: 517 681-3536

Mon. to Sat. 10 to 5, Sun. 12 to 5

2 miles east of U.S. 27, north side of street.

Furniture and a general
line of antiques.

Dealer space available.

5.4 Saginaw County

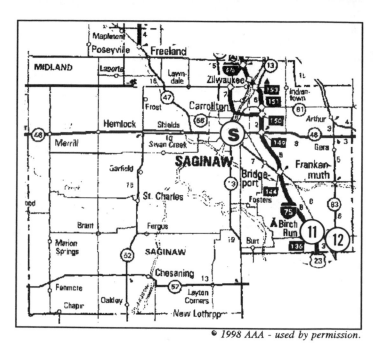

S = Saginaw: 4 - 8

CHESANING

1   Fancy That Antiques & Uniques
324 West Broad Street
Chesaning MI 48616
517 845-7775

2   The Place
210 West Broad Street
Chesaning MI 48616
517 327-5342
Crafts, collectibles, a few antiques.

ST. CHARLES

3   Judy's Treasures
11209 Prior
St. Charles MI 48655
517 865-9843

SAGINAW

4 Antique Warehouse
1910 North Michigan Ave. at Genesee
Saginaw MI 48602
517 755-4343
Mon. to Sat. 10 to 5, Sun. 12 to 5;
Nov. 15 to Jan. 1: Open to 6 daily.
I-75 to I-675 to Exit 3. (2 blocks off I-675). Northbound: Exit
left on Michigan. Southbound: Exit on Hill to Genesee - left
to N. Michigan. Eastbound & Westbound: Route 46 to
Michigan - turn north.
85 dealers, 30,000 square feet, cafe & specialty shoppes.

5 Adomaitis Antiques
412 Court Street
Saginaw MI 48600
517 790-7469
Mon. to Sat. 10:30 to 5
Historic Old Saginaw City.
Vintage clothing, jewelry, estate sales
In business 25 years.

6 Little House Antiques
418 Court Street
Saginaw MI 48602
517 799-4110
Wed. to Sat. 11 to 4
In Historic Old Saginaw City.
Depression Glass, kitchenware, elegant glass, collectibles, etc.

Map of Saganaw:

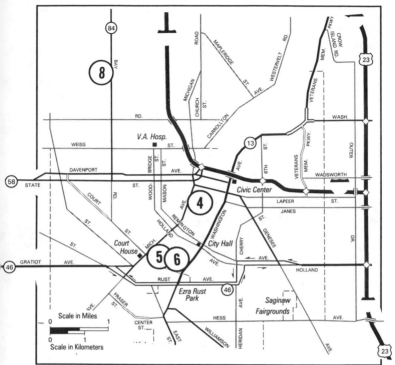

© *1998 AAA - used by permission.*

7   The Red Wagon
112 South Hamilton
Saginaw MI 48602
517 799-9667   Crafts, antiques & reproduction items.

8   Somewhere in Time Antiques & Collectibles Mall
Bay Square Shopping Center
2885 Bay Road
Saginaw MI 48603
517 497-7880
Mon. to Thurs. 10 to 6; Fri. & Sat. 10 to 8
From I-75 take the I-675 exit to the Davenport exit (#3), west to
Bay Road (M-84). Turn right (north) 1/4 mile to Mall.
6,200 square feet.   A fine selection of quality antiques and
collectibles. Seeking additional dealers; accepting quality
consignments. V/MC/D/AE

9   Ron's Antiques
12025 Gratiet Road. west of M-52
Saginaw (Hemlock) MI 48609   517 642-8479

FRANKENMUTH

10   B-C Antiques
8470 West Tuscola Road
Frankenmuth MI 48734
517 652-2116

BIRCH RUN

**11   The Collector's
Corner**

11900 South Gera
Road (MI Route 83)

Birch Run MI 48415

517 624-4388

Every Day 10 to 5

One block north of
Birch Run Road, west
side of highway.

**12   Red Beard's
Antiques &
Collectibles**

12025 North Gera
Road
Birch Run MI 48415

517 624-5211

Daily 10 to 6

ANTIQUES & COLLECTIBLES

Take a walk through time
at:

COLLECTOR'S CORNER

"The Cookie Jar Connection"
11900 S. Gera Rd. (M-83)
Birch Run, Michigan
517-624-4388
Open: 7 Days   Call for hours
2 mi. E. of I-75 exit 136
4 mi. S of Frankenmuth
Charge / Layaway / Ship

Southeast corner Gera & Birch Run Roads, south of
Frankenmuth.

"We buy old stuff."

MERRILL

13   Tillie's Treasures
M-46 West
Merrill MI 48637
517 643-7516

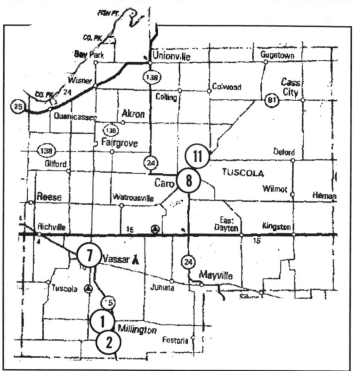

© 1998 AAA - used by permission.

MILLINGTON

1   Millington Antique Depot
8484 State Street
Millington MI 48746
517 871-3300; Fax: 517 871-7228
www.millingtonantiques.com
Sun. to Thurs. 10 to 5, Fri. & Sat. 10 to 6
Downtown, west side of the street.
Quality furniture and other antiques.

2   Millington Antique Co-Op Mall
8549 State Street (M-15)
Millington MI 48746
517 871-4597
Every day 10 to 6; Dec. 26 to April: open 12 to 5
East side of street, a block south of the Millington Antique
Depot.
Large mall; good quality furniture, pottery, antiques, and
collectibles.

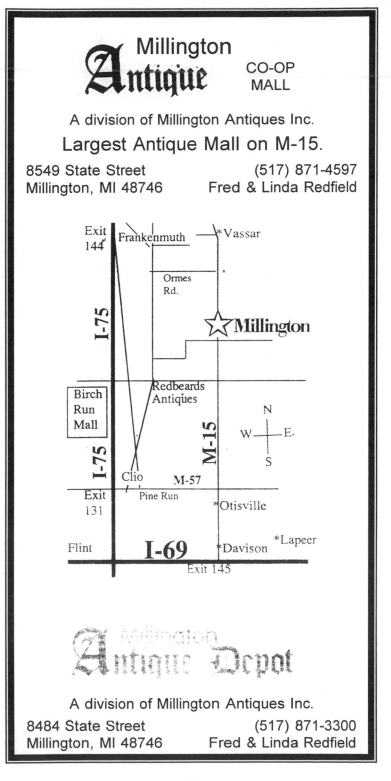

Millington

Antique CO-OP MALL

A division of Millington Antiques Inc.

Largest Antique Mall on M-15.

8549 State Street
Millington, MI 48746

(517) 871-4597
Fred & Linda Redfield

A division of Millington Antiques Inc.

8484 State Street
Millington, MI 48746

(517) 871-3300
Fred & Linda Redfield

3   Enduring Reflections
8516 State Street
Millington MI 48746   517 871-5080

4   Jim's Antiques
8590 State Street, in back of Country Shops gift & craft store.
Millington MI 48746   517 871-3523

5   Mike's Antiques and Old Goodies
5732 West Millington Road
Millington MI 48746
Evenings & weekends; days by chance.
West from the light Two miles.
Furniture refinished and in the rough; tall oak beds & farm
wagons always on hand.

VASSAR

6   Village Antiques & Collectibles
231 Goodrich Street (M-15 South)
Vassar MI 48768   517 823-3003

7   Weathervane Antique Emporium
135 East Huron Avenue
Vassar MI 48768
517-823-3181
Wed. to Sat. 10 to 4
Downtown
Coca Cola collectibles, Red Wing Pottery, Depression Glass, etc.

CARO

8   Quilt Talk Antiques
209 North State St.
Caro MI 48723
517 673-7994
Tues. to Sat. 10 to 5 - plus by special appointment.
M-24 to M-81 (or I-75 to M-81.)
2,200 sq. ft. of furniture, lamps, quilts, etc.   "Arranged to
enjoy, priced to sell."   Also: Quilt classes; 2 hours - $10.00.

9   This That and Then Some
1146 Caro, northeast on M-81
Caro MI 48723

10   Imperfections
113 North State Street
Caro MI 48723

11   Gallery Unique
1333 East Caro Road
Caro MI 48723
517 673-5118
Mon. to Sat. by chance or appointment.
Northeast end of town, northwest side of highway, a mile and
a half northeast of M-24. Store is next to the house.
Fine quality antiques.

——————   **KINGSTON**   ——————

12   Barron's Antiques
5969 State Street (M-46)
Kingston MI 48741   517 683-2750

SELECTED ANTIQUE SHOWS IN MICHIGAN
1999 SCHEDULE

Ann Arbor Antiques Market
5055 Ann Arbor-Saline Road, Ann Arbor, I-94 Exit 175, then south
three miles.   Admission $5.00, free parking.
April 17 & 18; May 16; June 20; July 18; August 15; September
18 & 19; October 17; November 7

Ludington Area Antique Shows
West Shore Community College, 3000 N. Stiles Road, Scottville.   616
845-7414 or 616 845-0450   Sat. 9 to 6, Sun. 11 to 4.
Winter Fun Fest: Feb. 6-7; Fall Festival: Oct. 16-17

Southfield Pavilion Antiques Exposition
Evergreen Road & 10 1/2 Mile Road; I-696 Exit 11 South
Fri. 2 to 9, Sat. 12 to 8, Sun. 12 to 5
Feb. 26-27-28 and Sept. 24-24-26;   Home & Garden Antique Market:
Mar. 19-20-21; Modernism Exposition: April 19-20-21;
Americana Antiques Show: Nov. 19 & 20

Utica Antiques Market
Knights of Columbus Grounds, 21 Mile Road, a mile east of Van
Dyke,   May 8-9, July 10-11, Sept. 11-12.   800 653-6466

Allegan Antique Market
Allegan County Fairgrounds in Allegan.   Last Sunday of the month
April through Sept.   616 453-8730 or 616 887-7677

Michigan Antique Festivals
Midland Fairgrounds, U.S. 10 at Eastman Ave.   517 687-9001
Antiques, folk art, auto display, free appraisal area.
June 5-6, July 24-25, Sept. 25-26

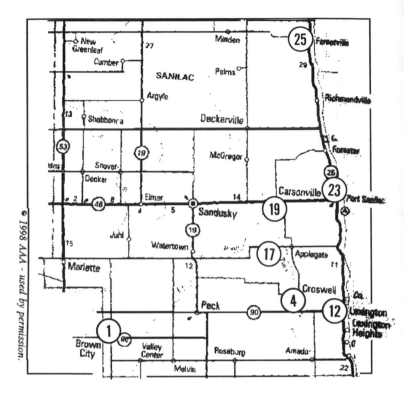

BROWN CITY

1   Pastime Treasures Antiques
4217 Main Street (M-90)
Brown City MI 48416
810 346-2254
Tues. to Fri. 9 to 4, Sat. 9 to 3
Downtown, south side of street.
Glassware, furniture, & general line of antiques.

2   Antiques Barn - Outback
Main & St. Mary's Streets
Brown City MI 48416
810 346-2331

CROSWELL

3   Neal's Floral Shop & Antiques
14 N. Howard Ave.
Croswell MI 48422   810 679-3554   Flowers; a few antiques.

4   Granny's Attic
27 South Howard Street
Croswell MI 48422
810 679-2975   810 359-7563
Sun. & Mon. 11 to 5; Sun. only in winter; or by appointment.
East side of street, three blocks north of M-90.   Croswell is
four miles west of Lexington.
General line, furniture, pottery, glassware, etc.

5   Black River Hobbies
80 North Howard Avenue
Croswell MI 48422
810 679-4750
Old electric trains.

6   Allen & Louise Dodd
4691 Croswell Road
Croswell MI 48422
810 679-2936

━━━━━   **LEXINGTON**   ━━━━━

7   Village House Antiques
5666 Main Street
Lexington MI 48450
810 359-7733
Weekends by chance.

8   Hunter House
5654 Main Street (M-25)
Lexington MI 48450
810 359-8016
Furniture - oak and primitives.

9   Time Will Tell
7245 Huron Avenue, west of M-25
Lexington MI 48450
810 359-2046   Clocks, clock repair, Fiesta, furniture, etc.

10   Bob Hobbs Gifts & Antiques
7262 Huron Street
Lexington MI 48450
810 359-8386

11   B. R. Noble Antiques
7247 Huron Avenue
Lexington MI 48450
810 359-2678
Furniture, lighting, reproductions. Proposed to open 1999.

12   The Emporium
7296 Huron Ave.
Lexington MI 48422
810 359-8033
Sun. to Fri. 11 to 5
Antiques, collectibles, and gifts.
Downtown, across from the post office.

13   Alison's Antique Antics
5184 South Lakeshore
Lexington MI 48422
810 359-2991

LEXINGTON HEIGHTS

14   Rare Earth Antiques
105 Fairbanks
Lexington Heights MI 48401   810 359-5966

APPLEGATE

15   Carol's Antiques
Main Street
Applegate MI 48401
810 679-3399

16   Julia Ostrowski Antiques
4762 Main Street
Applegate MI 48401
810 633-9479

17   Discover An Antique
4371 Applegate Road
Applegate MI 48401
810 633-9361 or 810 359-8972
Sat. 11 to 5
From Applegate go west on Applegate Road across the Black
River. In an old school house, north side of the road.   Look
for the "School's Open" flag.
The furniture restoration business is at 6901 Mortimer Lane.

CARSONVILLE

18   Jan's Antiques
560 Goetze Road
Carsonville MI 48419
810-657-9786
E-mail: jantique@greatlakes.net

19   Heritage Antiques
2692 North Lakeshore Road
Carsonville MI 48419
810 622-8003
May Through Oct.: Thur., Fri. and Sat. 11 to 5
North of Port Sanilac on M-25.
General line.

PORT SANILAC

20   Sarah's Colony & Crown Antiques
173 South Ridge (M-25)
Port Sanilac MI 48469
810 622-9020

21   Old Red Barn Antiques
235 Ridge Road (M-25)
Port Sanilac MI 48469   810 622-8297

22   Gull Cottage Antiques
2096 S. Lakeshore (M-25)
Port Sanilac
810 622-9883

23   Lalla Rookh Antiques
185 North Ridge Road (M-25)
Port Sanilac MI 48469
810 622-7966
Weekends
Three blocks north of the light, west side of the street.
Furniture, including mission & lodge look.

SANDUSKY

24   Back Alley Antiques Etc.
17 Lincoln Street
Sandusky MI 48471
810 648-5084

FORESTVILLE

25   Farmhouse Antiques
7914 Lake Road
Forestville MI 48225
517 864-5534
May 30 to Oct. 30: Sat. & Sun. 11 to 5
Off M-25 behind St. John's Catholic Church on Lake Huron.
Depression glass, fiestaware, pottery, 30's & 40's kitchen
collectibles, oak furniture.

TIER 6:
THE M-20 ROUTE

6.1 Oceana County

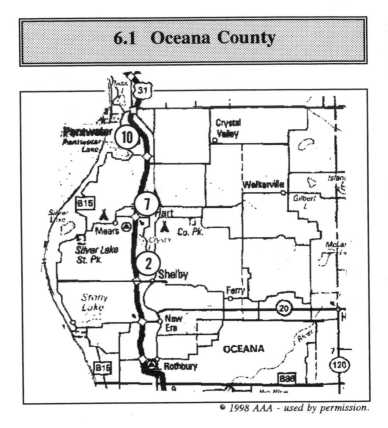

© *1998 AAA - used by permission.*

ROTHBURY

1   Oceana Antiques
6402 South Oceana Drive, north of town at Cleveland
Rothbury   MI 49452
616 861-4993

SHELBY

2   Nielsen's Nest
1021 South Oceana Dr. (Old U.S. 31)
Shelby   MI 49455
616 861-4920
May through Oct.: 10 to 5 Daily; Closed Sunday; Thurs. by
chance.
A half mile north of Shelby, west side of the highway.
Three large buildings in back of house. Furniture, glassware, etc.

3   The Barn Antiques
141 South 24th Avenue
Shelby   MI 49455
616 861-5038

MEARS

4   Remains to be Seen
56th & Taylor
Mears   MI 49436
616 873-3052

5   Silver Hills Antique Mall
6780 West Fox Road
Mears   MI 49436
616 873-3905

HART

6   Courtland House
16 Courtland Street
Hart   MI 49420
616 873-4746

7   The Flower Bin
27 South State Street
Hart   MI 49420
616 873-0222
Mon. to Sat. 10 to 6; Christmas through March: open special days
and by chance.
Downtown
Flowers and antiques.

8   Lakeview Antiques Plus
Main Street
Hart   MI 49420
616 873-8822

PENTWATER

9   The Berry Patch
218 South Hancock
Pentwater   MI 49449
616 869-5152
Gifts & a few antiques.

10   The Carriage House Antique Mall
50 Second Street
Pentwater MI 49449
616 869-0222
Mon. to Sat. 11 to 5, Sun. to 4; closed Christmas through March.
Half block east of Hancock St., in back of Painted Pony
Mercantile.
4,000 square foot multi-dealer shop.

6.2 Newaygo County

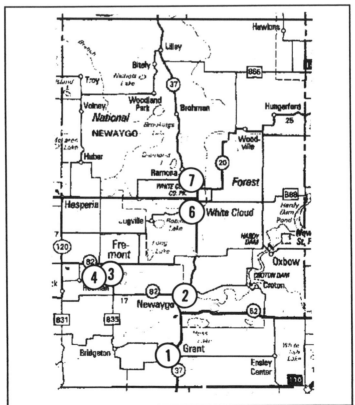

© *1998 AAA - used by permission.*

GRANT

1   Big Apple Antique Mall
86 North Maple
Grant MI 49327
616 834-8088; Fax: 616 887-9151
Mon. to Sat. 11 to 5, Fri. to 7; Sun. 1 to 5
East side of M-37, north of downtown.
Many dealers with full line of unique antiques and collectibles.

NEWAYGO

2   River Valley Antique Mall
41 State Road (M-37)
Newaygo MI 49337
616 652-4519
Mon. to Sat. 10:30 to 5:30, Sun. 1 to 4
Heart of Downtown Newaygo.
4,000 square feet floor space. Quality antiques, collectibles,
books, furniture, and primitives.

FREMONT

3   Rolling Ladders Antiques
10 East Main Street
Fremont MI 49412
616 924-0420
Mon. to Sat. 10 to 5:30. Sun. by chance or appointment.
Downtown at Division & Main.
General line.

4   Brass Bell Antique Mall
48 West Main
Fremont MI 49412
616 924-1255
Mon. to Sat. 10 to 5:30, Sun. 12 to 5
Downtown
Four showrooms of antiques, plus newly added Espresso Bar.

WHITE CLOUD

5   The Heritage Shop
2357 West One Mile Road (M-20)
White Cloud MI 49349
No telephone listed.

6   Beacon Lights
1165 Wilcox Avenue
White Cloud MI 49349
616 689-5122
Mon. to Sat. 10:30 to 5
Half block west of the light, north side of the street.
Books, maps, and assorted unusual items.
"Where it's usual to find the unusual."

7   Rosy Green's Antiques
901 North Evergreen (M-37)
White Cloud   MI 49349
616 689-5849
Thurs. to Sat. 10 to 5, Sun. 12 to 5
One mile north of White Cloud, west side of highway.
General line of antiques.

6.3 Mecosta County

© 1998 AAA - used by permission.

BIG RAPIDS

1 Big Rapids Antique Mall
107 S. Michigan
Big Rapids MI 49307
616 796-4100
Mon. to Sat. 10 to 5, most Sun. 12 to 4; Winter hours vary.
Downtown, one block east of Business Loop U.S. 131 in historic
Nisbett Building.
Specialties: oak furniture, knives, coins, vintage clothing, pottery
& glassware, books, toys, jewelry.

PARIS

2 R. & M. Log Cabin
22920 Northland Drive (Old 131)
Paris MI 49338
616 832-2941   New furniture & reproductions; few antiques.

3 Paris Country Shop
22203 Northland Drive (Old U.S. 131)
Paris   MI 49338   616 832-4533

MECOSTA

4 The Tamarack Shoppe Crafts & Collectiques
699 West Main Street (M-20)
Mecosta   MI 49332
616 972-4222
Fri., Sat. & Mon 10 to 5; Sun. 12 to 5
West of downtown, southeast corner Franklin and Main Streets.
Dolls, Furniture, quilts, depression, pattern & Fenton glass,
Griswold iron, lots of antiques and crafts. Layaways: 10% down,
10% a month.

6 The Browse Around
301 West Main Street (M-20)
Mecosta   MI 49332
616 972-2990; 616 972-8103   Antiques and used furniture.

REMUS

7 The Barn
231 East Wheatland (M-20 East)
Remus   MI 49340   517 967-3402

8 Wheatland Trading Post Craft & Antique Mall
298 W. Wheatland
Remus MI 49340
517 967-3400

197

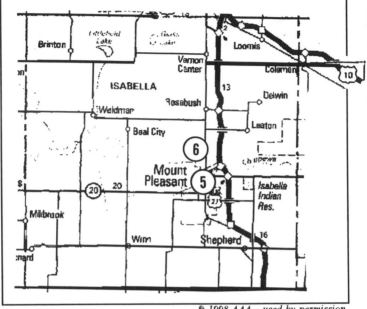

© 1998 AAA - used by permission.

BLANCHARD

1   Loafers Glory
431 Main Street
Blanchard   MI 49310
517 561-2020
Mostly gift items; a few antiques.

SHEPHERD

2   Bird House
320 West Wright
Shepherd MI 48883
517 828-5367
Gifts, antiques, dried flowers, crafts.

MT. PLEASANT

3   Antiques on the Side
1833 West Millbrook Road
Mt. Pleasant   MI 48858-8521
517 866-2527;   Fax: 517 866-2749
www.power-net.net/users/mi3120

4   Antiques Center of Mt. Pleasant
1718 South Mission, north of Broomfield
Mt. Pleasant   MI 48858
517 772-2672

5   Mt. Pleasant Antiques Market

319 North Mission
Mt. Pleasant MI 48858
517 779-0000
www.antiquemkt.com
Daily 10 to 6
North end of town at Lincoln & Mission, west side of the street,
across from the Pixi Restaurant.
10,000, square feet, soon to be expanded to 23,000 square feet.

6   Antiques & Collectibles

1005 North Mission
Mt. Pleasant MI 48858
517 772-0073
Daily 2 to 6
Just north of Meijer store go Left from Business U.S. 27 on
Mission; go 2 miles north to Jordon, then left.
Several pole barns behind the 1954 vintage house
Pottery, glassware, bottles, etc.

Map: City of Mt. Pleasant:

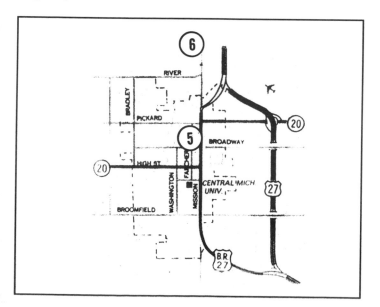

6.5 Midland County

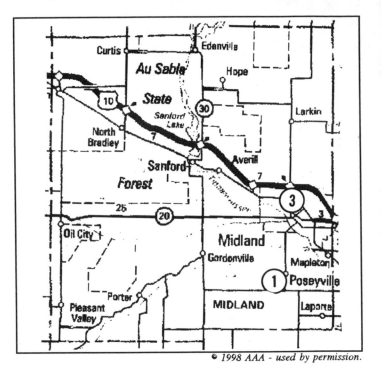

© 1998 AAA - used by permission.

MIDLAND

1 D.A.D.'s Antiques
3004 Poseyville Road
Midland MI 48640
517 835-7483
Wed. to Sun. 10 to 4
Corner Poseyville & Freeland Roads, 6 miles south of downtown.
General Line

2 Big Jim's Antiques
4816 Bay City Road, west of U.S. 10
Midland MI 48642
517 496-0734

3 King Solomon's
201 East Main Street
Midland MI 48640
517 837-5464
Mon. to Fri. 10 to 7, Sat. 10 to 5
Downtown, just east of M-20.
Gifts, Antiques, Christian books & Jewish items.

Map: City of Midland:

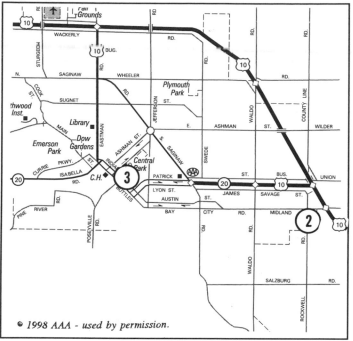

© 1998 AAA - used by permission.

4   Linda's Cobble Shop
2900 Isabella Street
Midland MI 48640
517 832-9788   Parking and entrance in rear.

5   Corner Cupboard
2112 East Wheeler Road
Midland MI 48642
517 835-6691

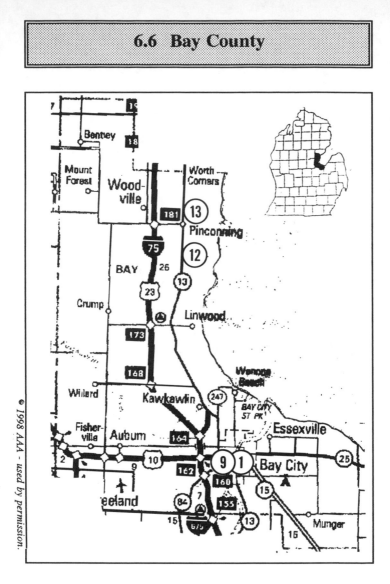

© 1998 AAA - used by permission.

BAY CITY

1 Bay City Antiques Center
1010 North Water Street
Bay City MI 48708
517 893-0251
www.antiquecenteronline.com
Mon. to Sat. 10 to 5, Fri. till 8; Sun. 12 to 5
Downtown, southeast corner Third & Water Streets. From 1-75:
Exit 162-A toward downtown, take the 1st left after river -
Saginaw Street; go 6 blocks north to 3rd, then left 1 block to
Water Street, then left. Entrance is under the blue awning.
53,000 square feet. Block long building with three floors. Enter
under the blue awning.   Always free coffee.

Map: Bay City:

® 1998 AAA - used by permission.

2   Ames Bargain Center
800 Garfield
Bay City MI 48706
517 892-4874

3   Mid Michigan Retail Sales
614 Garfield
Bay City MI 48706
517 893-6537   Antique used furniture & collectibles.

4   Little House
924 North Water
Bay City MI 48706
517 893-6771   Gifts, only a few antiques.

5   A Weathered Gate Antiques & Gifts
920 North Water
Bay City MI 48708
517 895-7902   Gifts, crafts, antiques.

6   Hen in the Holly
110 Third Street, between Water & Washington Streets
Bay City MI 48708
517 895-7215
Antiques and folk art.

7   Trinkets & Treasures
113 Third Street
Bay City MI 48708
517 893-7143

8   Cottage Thyme
207 3rd Street
Bay City MI 48708
517 892-0005

9   Everybody's Attic
606 East Midland Street
Bay City MI 48706
517 893-9702
Daily 11 to 5:30, closed Thurs.;
Nov. 1 to April 1: also closed Wed.
South side of street, 2 blocks west of the river in the Historic
West Side Midland District, one block south of the Vermont
Street bridge. Go south on Walnut after crossing bridge.

10   Owl Antiques
703 East Midland Street
Bay City MI 48706
517 892-1105

11   All American Trade Center
601 Euclid
Bay City MI 48706
Proposed to open in 1999.

PINCONNING

12   Northern Lights
1948 North Huron Road (M-13)
Pinconning MI 48650
517 879-6655
Mon. to Sat. 10 to 5, Sun. 12 to 5
Four miles south of Pinconning.
Complete general line of fine antiques, specializing in lamps and
dolls.

13   E & J Antique Mall
3726 North Huron Road (M-13)
Pinconning MI 48650
517 879-3300
E-mail: cjs@journys.com
Mon. to Sat. 10 to 5:30, Sun. 12 to 5
East side of the highway, 1/4 mile south of light.
Over 300 pieces of furniture; 7,000 square feet of antiques.
Complete restoration and repair services.

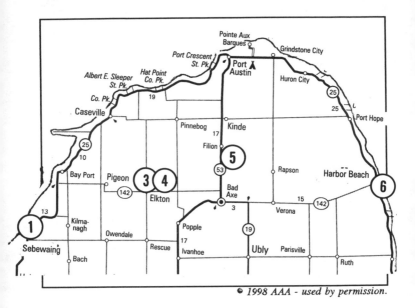

© 1998 AAA - used by permission.

SEBEWAING

1   Antiques By-The-Bridge
4 North Center Street
Sebewaing MI 48759
517 883-9424
Summer: Daily 10 to 5;
Rest of Year: Thurs. to Sat. 10 to 5, Sun. by chance.
Five large rooms full of antiques in renovated historic 1895
building. The Antique Inn Bed & Breakfast is located on the
second floor.

2   Past and Present Collectibles
622 Beck Street
Sebewaing MI 48759
517 883-2484

ELKTON

3   Antiques & More
36 North Main Street
Elkton MI 48731
517 375-2426
Fri. & Sat. 9:30 to 5
Downtown
10 dealers

4   Mckenzie's Gifts & Antiques

48 North Main Street
Elkton   MI 48731
517 375-2750
April to Jan.: Mon. to Sat. 9 to 5
Feb. to March: Fri. &   Sat. 9 to 5
Downtown, east side of street.
Furniture, glassware, jewelry, and collectibles.

BAD AXE

5   The Old Mill Antiques

M-53, P.O. Box 323
Bad Axe   MI 48413
517 269-9254
Seasonal, Summer 7 days, Fall 4 days, Winter Sat. & Sun.
Just south of Filion, 5 miles north of Bad Axe, southeast corner
Van Dyke (M-53) & Crown Road.
Antiques, collectibles, gifts, and an old-fashioned ice cream parlor
in season.

HARBOR BEACH

6   McGray's Antiques (2 shops)

230 North State Street (M-142)
Harbor Beach   MI 48441
517 479-3713
Daily Mon. to Sat. 10 to 5, Sun. 12 to 5;
South side of street.
Also a shop at 236 State Street.
Glassware, oak furniture, and a general line.

PORT HOPE

7   Port Hope Antiques, Collectibles & Crafts
Name to be changed in 1999.
4432 Main Street
Port Hope   MI 48441
No phone at press time.

TIER 7:
LUDINGTON-GLADWIN-
STANDISH

7.1 Mason County

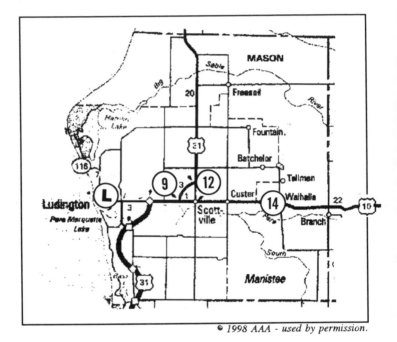

© 1998 AAA - used by permission.

L = Ludington: 1 - 8

LUDINGTON

1   Sandpiper Emporium
809 West Ludington Avenue, at Lakeshore Dr.
Ludington   MI 49431
616 843-3008
Antiques as part of gift & apparel shop in resort complex.
The antiques are in several rooms in back and to the left.

2   Country Charm
119 West Ludington Avenue
Ludington   MI 49431
616 843-4722   Gift shop, with a few antiques.

3   Cole's Antiques Villa
322 West Ludington Avenue
Ludington   MI 49431
616 845-7414
Summer: Mon. to Sat. 10 to 6, Sun. 12 to 5;
April to June: Mon. to Sat. 10 to 5, Sun. 12 to 5; closed
January to March.
West end of downtown, just east of the House of Flavors.
2,400 square feet. Quality furniture, pottery, glass, etc.

4   The Antique Store
127 South James, at Loomis
Ludington   MI 49431
616 845-5888; (708 852-8170 off season)

5   Sunset Bay Antiques
404 South James Street
Ludington   MI 49431
616 843-1559

6   Elliott's Antiques
900 South Washington
Ludington MI 49431
616 845-5944

7   Washington Antiques
1001 South Washington Avenue, at 2nd
Ludington   MI 49431
616 843-8030 Building for sale at time of survey; shop may
close.

8   Christa's Antiques & Collectibles
1002 South Madison, at 2nd
Ludington   MI 49431
616 845-0075

9   Always Antique Mall
2144 Johnson Road
Ludington MI 49431
616 843-8781
Summer: Every day 11 to 5;
Winter: Fri. to Sun. 11 to 5; closed Jan.
Midway between Ludington and Scottville go north on Styles
Street 1/4 mile to Johnson Road, then east 1/4 mile.
Furniture, glassware, etc.

SCOTTVILLE

10   Main Corner Antique Mall
101 North Main Street
Scottville   MI 49454
616 757-0262

11   Frick's Old Country Store
120 North Main Street, at Broadway
Scottville   MI 49454
616 757-4708

12   School House Antiques
2872 North U.S. 31
Scottville   MI 49454
616 757-9364
Usually Every Day 10 to 5
Northeast corner Sugar Grove   & U.S. 31, 3 miles north of
Scottville.
Primitives, country, windmills, etc.

FREE SOIL

13   Country Style Antiques
6601 Stephens Road
Free Soil   MI 49411
616 462-3706

WALHALLA

14   Olde Friends Antiques & Collectibles
6796 East U.S. 10
Walhalla MI 49410
616 757-3081
May to Oct.: Thurs. to Mon. 10 to 5; April: open weekends
only; closed Dec. to March.
North side of the highway at the curve, 22 miles east of
Ludington.
General line of antiques.

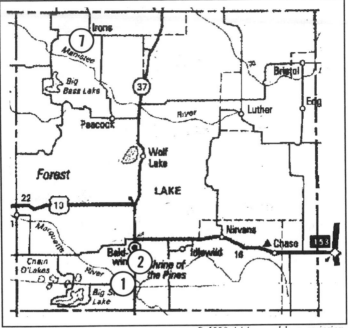

© *1998 AAA - used by permission.*

BALDWIN

1   Paul Bunyan Antiques Mall
3253 South M-37
Baldwin   MI 49304
616 745-2637
Daily Mid-March to Mid-Nov.
Evenings and winter weekends by chance or appointment.
3 miles south of Baldwin, west side of highway.

2   River Bend Trading Post
300 Michigan Avenue (M-37 South)
Baldwin   MI 49304
616 745-4030
April to Labor Day: daily 11 to 5;
Labor Day to Dec.: Sat. & Sun. 11 to 5
Northeast corner M-37 & Carroll's Trail
Antiques, collectibles, and antique hunting & fishing items.

3   Baldwin Department Store
876 North Michigan
Baldwin MI 49304   616 745-3101

CHASE

4   A & A Chase Country Store
100 Main Street
Chase   MI 49623
616 832-3356

LUTHER

5   Hopeful Antiques
6330 Skookum Road
Luther   MI 49656
616 829-3977
Between Luther and Bristol, 10 miles west of U.S. 131.

IRONS

6   Wheeler Dealer Store
10 1/2 Mile Road
Irons   MI 49644
616 266-5521
A few antiques might be available at the lumber yard.

7   Antiques on the Corner
10486 Brook Road
Irons MI 49644
616 266-6111
April to November: Thurs. & Fri. 10 to 5, Sat. 10 to 6,
Sun. 10 to 3
Downtown Irons, at 10 1/2 Mile Road.
Furniture, primitives, glassware, and general line.

ARTS & CRAFTS MOVEMENT ON THE INTERNET

There are many internet sites related to various aspects of the Arts
and Crafts Movement and mission oak furniture. Fortunately there
are several sites offering assistance in finding them.   The first is
Web Links: Arts & Crafts on the web at:

> http://pwl.netcom/~shura/web-links.html

The Arts & Crafts Movement Review is another internet source for
arts & crafts enthusiasts: http://pwl.netcom.com/~shura/main.html

The Arts & Crafts Society website (www.arts-crafts.com) has five
sections: Archives, Bookstore, Events, Forum, and Marketplace.
This site provides a good introduction to the history, philosophy,
and design of the Arts & Crafts Movement.

7.3 Osceola County

Map: Oscoda & Clare Counties:

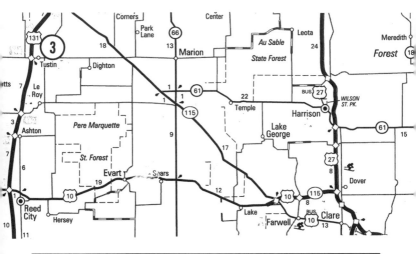

© 1998 AAA - used by permission.

EVART

1   LC's Chicken Coop
1014 North M-66, between 12 & 13 Mile Roads.
Evart   MI 49631
616 743-2456

MARION

2   Good Friend's Antiques and Flea Market
15396 M-115, north of M-66
Marion   MI 49665   616 743-6173

TUSTIN

3   Pine River Antiques
105 Church Street
Tustin MI 49688
616 829-4767
E-mail: jballoff@michweb.net
June to Oct.: Wed. to Sat. 11 to 4
U.S. 131 Exit 168; Downtown.
General line.

4 High Button Shoe
19338 19 Mile Road
Tustin MI 49688
616 829-3308

7.4 Clare County

> Map on Preceding Page <

CLARE

5 House of Antiques & Collectibles
10472 South Clare Avenue (Old U.S. 27)
Clare MI 48617
517 386-3571   Glassware, dolls, etc.

HARRISON

6 Antique Marketing Co. (aka Lott's Antiques)
7112 West Temple Drive (M-61)
Harrison MI 48625
616 743-6222   10 miles west of Harrison.

7.5 Gladwin County

BEAVERTON

1   The Trumpeter
104 West Brown
Beaverton MI 48612
517 435-4719
Tues. to Sat. 10 to 5, Fri. to 5:30
Downtown, just west of M-18, next to the B.T.
Anne of Green Gables merchandise, Yankee Candles,
Heritage Lace, and other gifts and antiques.

2   Golden Oaks
4568 M-30
Beaverton MI 48612
517 435-4838   Gifts, a few antiques.

Map: Gladwin County:

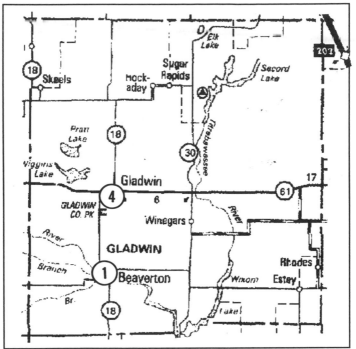

© 1998 AAA - used by permission.

GLADWIN

3   Cathy's Crafts & Collectibles
212 West Cedar
Gladwin MI 48624
517 426-4181

4   Passin' Time
225 West Cedar Avenue (the main street)
Gladwin MI 48624
517 426-7823
Tue. to Fri. 9 to 5, Sat. 9 to 12
Downtown, south side of street.
Clocks and clock repair. Also furniture restoration and
restored antiques.

5   The Antique Mall
125 Cedar Avenue (M-61)
Gladwin MI 48624
517 426-9221

7.6 Arenac County

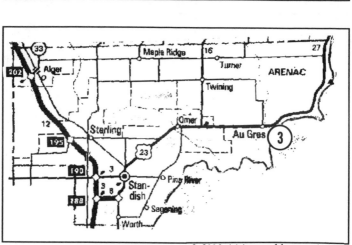

© *1998 AAA - used by permission.*

OMER

1   Quilt Patch Antiques
429 East Center (U.S. 23)
Omer MI 48749
517 653-2332

AU GRES

2   Nicks Wood Shop
134 Michigan Avenue
Au Gres MI 48703
517 876-7075

3   The Second Time Around
611 East Michigan Ave.
Au Gres MI 48703
517 876-7413
Every day 10 to 5
At H & H Restaurant & Bakery on U.S. 23 turn south on
Main; go 2 blocks to Michigan and turn left (east). Big white
house surrounded by white picket fence.
Glassware, china, collectibles.

STANDISH

4   The Up North Store
201 South Main
Standish MI 48658   517 846-4633

TIER 8:
THE M-55 ROUTE

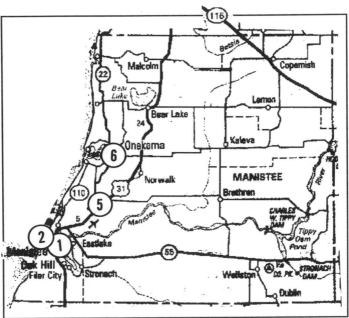

© 1998 AAA - used by permission.

MANISTEE

1   Antiques & Uniques
351 River Street
Manistee   MI 49660
616 398-9339
May to Oct.: Mon. to Sat. 10 to 5; Sun. 12 to 5;
call for winter hours.
Downtown, north side of the street.
Note: River Street is one-way west-bound.

2   River Street Antiques
382 River Street
Manistee   MI 49660
616 723-9133
Summer: Mon. & Wed.- Sat.: 11 - 8, Tues. 11 - 5; Sun. 12 - 4;
Winter: Mon., Thurs. & Sat.: 11 - 5; Fri. 11 - 8; Sun. 12 - 4
Downtown, south side of the street.
All types of antiques, furniture, primitives, pottery, glassware.

3 Cornerstone Antiques & Collectibles
399 River Street, AT Maple
Manistee   MI 49660
616 398-9089

4 Victoria's Attic & Arbor
113 Washington Street, north of the river
Manistee   MI 49660
616 723-5183
Antiques, reproductions, garden trellis.

5 North Country Antiques
3376 Chippewa Highway (U.S. 31 North)
Manistee   MI 49660
616 723-5675
Open all year by chance or appointment.
7 miles north of Manistee, house on west side of highway.
General line of antiques; furniture and glass. Also antique restoration.

ONEKAMA

6 The Old Farm Store
8011 First Street
Onekama   MI 49675
616 889-3733
Memorial Day to Labor Day: Mon. to Sat. 10 to 4.
Northeast corner M-22 & 8 Mile Road, south end of town, 1 1/4 mile west of U.S. 31.
Art, antiques, Americana.

7 Country Corner
5119 Main Street
Onekama   MI 49675
616 889-4451

8 Main Street Mall
4987 Main Street
Onekama MI 49675
616 889-5480

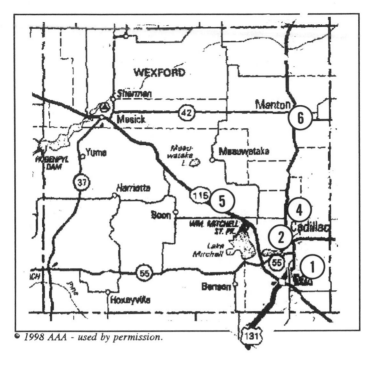

© 1998 AAA - used by permission.

CADILLAC

1 Phyllis' Olde House Antiques
7803 South 45 Mile Road
Cadillac   MI 49601
616 775-7502
Year round by chance or appointment, closed Saturdays.
From Cadillac: East 2 miles East-southeast from US 131 at
State Police Light, around the bend; on the east side of the
road, one door south of Fox TV.
Shop in home; general line with glassware, china, smalls plus
furniture.

2 Downtown Antiques & Collectibles
215 North Mitchell Street
Cadillac   MI 49601
616 876-2399
Mon. to Sat. 10 to 5
Downtown, lower level of Mitchell Street Lighting, next to
Sears.
General line of antiques, plus collectibles and gifts.

3   Scholten's Antiques
10600 East Division
Cadillac   MI 49601
616 775-7504
2 miles east of Cadillac on M-55 at Hemlock Drive.

4   Royer's Antique Mall
211 Bell Avenue
Cadillac MI 49601
616 779-2434
Mon. to Sat. 10 to 5; also Sun. 12 to 5 in summer.
North two miles on U.S. 131 to Wendy's Restaurant, east one-half block, north side of street.
Depression glass, fishing collectibles, pottery, toys, and general line.

5   Thomason's Antiques
740 North 29 Mile Road
Cadillac MI 49601
616 775-0028
Daily 10 to 6, year-round.
Quarter mile south of Meauwataka Store, or 3.5 miles north of M-115.
General line of quality antiques: glass, china, pottery, jewelry, furniture, etc.

MANTON

6   Manton Antiques
212 S. Michigan (U.S. 131)
Manton   MI 49663
616 824-3783,   E-mail: anna@northlink.net
Tue. to Sat. 9 to 5
Northwest corner Williams Street, 2 blocks south of downtown.
Furniture; collectible teddy bears; hardware; toy trains; Beanie Babies.

MESICK

7   Hide-Away Antiques and Sugar Bush
9431 N 13 Mile (M-37)
Mesick   MI 48668
616 885-2900   Primitives and collectibles

8   Family Tree Antiques
1599 Old M-37
Mesick   MI 49668   616 389-0079

8.3 Missaukee County

© 1998 AAA - used by permission.

LAKE CITY

1   Larry's Used and Antiques
838 North Morey Road (M-66)
Lake City   MI 49651
616 839-4210

2   Lake City Flea Market
518 East Union
Lake City   MI 49651
616 839-3206

8.4 Roscommon County

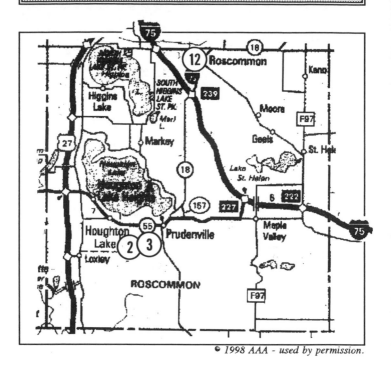

© 1998 AAA - used by permission.

HOUGHTON LAKE

1   A Summer Place
6415 West Houghton Lake Drive (Old Highway 55)
Houghton Lake MI 48629   517 422-6030

2   Henry's Antiques
Loxley Road
Houghton Lake MI 48629
517 422-4771
Mon. Tues. Fri. & Sat. 10 to 5
From U.S. 27: East on M-55 to Loxley (2nd blinker light),
then south one mile; east side of the road.
Furniture, glassware, collectibles, antique sporting items, etc.

3   Maxine's Antiques
7821 Stone School Road
Houghton Lake MI 48629
517 422-5751
Mon. to Sat. 9 to 4
From Old 27 east on M-55 1.4 miles to Loxley Road, then
south .5 mile to Stone School Road, then east .2 mile.
Good quality furniture.

4   Berta's Antiques and Collectible Mall
6970 West Houghton Lake Drive (M-55), west of Loxley Rd.
Houghton Lake   MI 48629
517 422-5298

5   Macvicar Antiques
9103 West Haughton Lake Drive
Houghton Lake   MI 48629
517 422-5466

━━━━━━━━━━ **PRUDENVILLE** ━━━━━━━━━━

6   Iron Kettle
931 West houghton Lake Drive (M-55)
Prudenville MI 48651

7   The Carousel Shoppe
1460 West Houghton Lake Drive, at Iroquois
Prudenville MI 48651
517 366-5477   Gifts, crafts, antiques.

━━━━━━━━━━ **ROSCOMMON** ━━━━━━━━━━

8   Antique Cupboard
M-18
Roscommon MI 48653

9   Finders Keepers
M-18
Roscommon MI 48653
517 275-5650

10   Broken Wheel
M-76
Roscommon MI 48653

11   Yorty's Antiques
103 Yorty Drive (West Higgins Lake Drive)
Roscommon MI 48653
517 821-9242

12   Apples & Spice
406 A N. 5th Street
Roscommon MI 48653
517 275-2028
Summer: Daily 10 to 6; Winter: closed Tues.
Downtown.
Antiques, gifts, collectibles, and unique items.

8.5 Ogemaw County

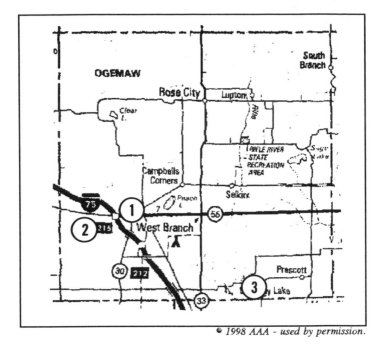

© 1998 AAA - used by permission.

WEST BRANCH

1 The Potato Barn Antique Mall
615 West Houghton
West Branch MI 48661
517 343-3333
Tues. to Sat. 10 to 5, Sun. 12 to 5
Downtown, north side of the street, behind the China Inn
Restaurant.
General line of antiques and collectibles.

2 The Cocklebur
2161 Pointer Road
West Branch MI 48661
517 345-7242
E-Mail: cocklebur@juno.com
April 15 to Dec. 31: Wed. to Fri. 10 to 5, Sat. 10 to 4,
Sun. & holidays by chance.
1 mile west and 1/8 mile south of I-75 Exit 215.
Primitives, glassware, jewelry, furniture, trunks, miscellaneous.

PRESCOTT

3   Hilltop House Antiques
2016 East M-55
Prescott MI 48756
517 345-3540; 517 345-7242
May 1 to Nov. 1: Wed. to Sun. 12 to 5;
Winter: Sat. & Sun. 10 to 5
South side of highway at Peterson Road, 4 miles east of MI
33.
Expert clock repair & collectibles.

8.6 Iosco County

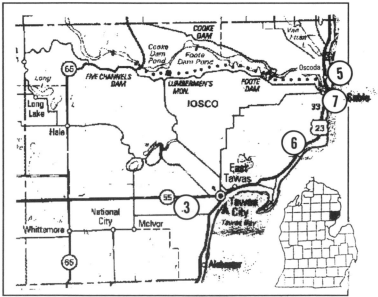

© 1998 AAA - used by permission.

TAWAS CITY

1   Alabaster Corners
2441 Huron
Tawas City MI 48763
517 362-7777   Gifts, collectibles, antiques, candles.

2   Uncle Winnies
402 Lake Street (U.S. 23), in the Liberty Building
Tawas City MI 48764
517 362-6644

3   Time After Time Antiques
729 M-55 West
Tawas City MI 48763
517 362-2298
E-mail: eternity@i-star.com
Fri. thru Tues. 10 to 5, Wed. & Thurs. by appointment.
Two miles west of U.S. 23.
Glassware, furniture, primitives, vintage jewelry, collectibles,
and much much more.   Visa, Master Card and Discovery
Cards honored; gift certificates available.

OSCODA

4   Wooden Nickel Antiques
110 Park
Oscoda MI 48750
517 739-7490

5   Ryland Co. Clocks and Antiques
2091 N. U.S. 23
Oscoda MI 48750
517 739-0810
Wed. to Sun. 11 to 5
5.5 miles south of Oscoda, across from Point Road.

6 McNamara Antique Mall
2083 North U.S. 23
Oscoda MI 48750
517 739-5435
Summer: Every day 11 to 4;
Winter: Fri. through Mon. 11 to 4
On U.S. 23 halfway between Tawas and Oscoda.
Antiques, collectibles, primitives. Outdoor yard ornaments.

7 Hobart's Antique Mall
4219 U.S. 23
Oscoda MI 48730
517 739-4000
Summer: Every day 10 to 5;
Winter: Fri. to Sun. 11 to 5, or by appointment.
In the back right corner of a complex of buildings, 1.7 miles
south of downtown, west side of highway.
Reproductions in the front building, antiques & collectibles in
the back building, plus a barn full of refinished furniture.

8 Powers Antiques
7324 Loud Drive
Oscoda MI 48750
517 739-1840
3 miles north of tracks off Cedar Lake Road.

9 Mill Street Antiques
State Street
Oscoda MI 48750
No telephone listed.

HALE

10 Elsie's Hale Creek Antiques
201 North Washington (M-65)
Hale MI 48739
517 728-2538

11 Mary's Hope Chest
6625 M-65
Hale MI 48739
517 728-2888
5.5 miles north of town.

TIER 9:
THE M-72 ROUTE

9.1 Benzie County

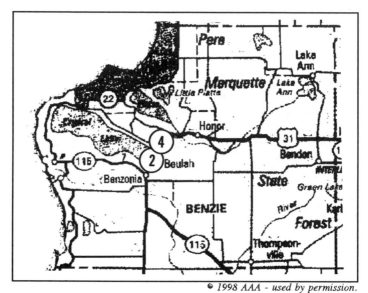

FRANKFORT

1   Frankfort Antique Market
735 Main Street
Frankfort MI 49635
616 352-7707

BEULAH

2   Myers Granary Antique Market
7300 Crystal Avenue
Beulah MI 49617
616 882-4299
May to Oct.: Mon. to Sat. 10 to 5, Sun. 12 to 5
Downtown Beulah, on the new Trail.
General line of antiques.

3   Crystal Lake Antiques
244 South Benzie
Beulah MI 49617
616 882-5081

4   Black Horse Antiques
11 North Benzie Boulevard
Beulah MI 49617
No telephone in shop.
May to Sept.: Mon. to Sat. 10 to 5
Three blocks north of downtown.

HONOR

5   Red Sled Antiques
10956 Main Street (U.S. 31)
Honor MI
616 325-3275

9.2 Leelanau County

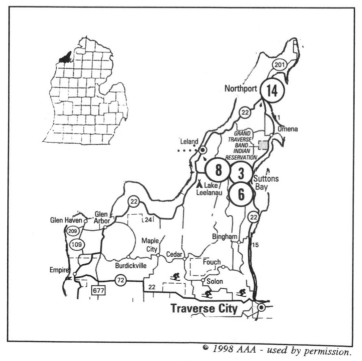

© *1998 AAA - used by permission.*

SUTTONS BAY

1   Sutton's Bay Galleries
102 Jefferson Street
Suttons Bay   MI 49682
616 271-4444
16th - 20th Century Fine Art and Antiquarian Prints.

2   Applegate Collection
405 St. Joseph Avenue
Suttons Bay   MI 49682
616 271-5252
Gifts, housewares, antiques.

3   Danbury Antiques
305 St. Joseph Avenue
Suttons Bay   MI 49682
616 271-3211
May to Oct.: Mon. to Sat. 10 to 6; Sun. 12 to 4;
rest of year by chance or appointment.
Downtown
English smalls.

4   Borgeau-Richards Collection
309 St. Joseph Avenue
Suttons Bay   MI 49682
616 271-2620   Gifts, housewares, antiques.

5   Up North Antiques
311 North Street
Suttons Bay   MI 49682
616 271-5400

6   Eagles Roost Antiques
5046 West Bay Shore
Suttons Bay   MI 49682
616 271-4807
Feb. to Nov.: Wed. to Sat. 10 to 5;
Jan. by chance or appointment; closed Dec.
South to party store; down Shady Lane.
Country, primitives, accessories.

LAKE LEELANAU

7   Cabbages and Kings
461 Main Street (M-204)
Lake Leelanau MI 49653
616 256-7913   general line; Depression Glass; and gifts.

8 Lake Leelanau Antiques
102 Meinard Street
Lake Leelanau MI 49653
616 256-7951
Memorial Day through Oct.: Tues. - Sat. 10 - 5, Sun. 12 4;
Nov. through Jan.: Fri. & Sat. 11 - 5, Sun. 12 - 4;
closed Feb. to Memorial Day.
West over the bridge, then south one block on St. Mary's
Street, then right on Meinard Street; blue building on the
corner.
Furniture, European antique, collectibles.

LELAND

9 The Old Library
103 East River Street
Leland   MI 49654
616 256-7428
Seasonal   Across from historic Bluebird Restaurant.

NORTHPORT

10 Fifth Street Antiques
201 Mill Street (M-201)
Northport   MI 49670
616 386-5421

11 Cobweb Treasures
393 West Street
Northport   MI 49670
616 386-5532
E-Mail: cobweb@traverse.com
1 block west of M-22/201 light, first house.

12 Manitou Gallery
210 Mill Street
Northport   MI 49670
New shop proposed to open in 1999.

13 Bird-n-Hand
123 Nagonaba
Northport   MI 49670
Near the harbor, next to the library.

14 Back Roads Antiques
116 East Nagonaba
Northport MI 49670
616 386-7011

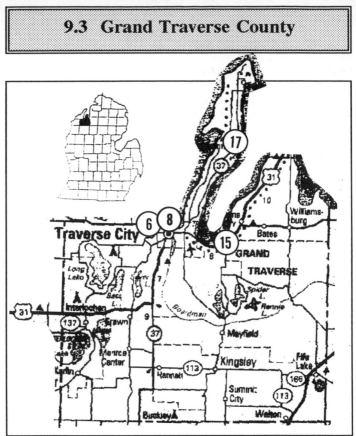

© 1998 AAA - used by permission.

KINGSLEY

1   B & E Antiques
260 East Main (M-113)
Kingsley MI 49649
616 263-7677

INTERLOCHEN

2   Betsie-Bo's Antiques
6470 Betsie River Road
Interlochen   MI 49643
616 276-9514

3   The Miser's Hoard
9955 U.S. 31 South
Interlochen   MI 49643
616 276-7642
1/4 mile west of the Interlochen light, south side of highway.
Antiques, junk, era clothing and oddities.

TRAVERSE CITY

4   Chum's Corner Antique Mall
4200 US 31 South
Traverse City   MI 49684   616 943-4200

5   Antique Emporium
565 Blue Star Drive
Traverse City   MI 49684   616 943-3658

6   Rolling Hills Antiques
5085 Barney Road
Traverse City   MI 49684
616 947-1063
Every day 10 to 6, other times by appointment for serious
buyers.
From U.S. 31 near downtown: west on Randolph Street,
which becomes Barney Road.
Specializing in American furniture from 1800 to 1925, lighting
and accessories.   *"Great selection at reasonable prices."*
Credit cards accepted, free furniture delivery within 25 miles.

7   Custer Antiques
826 West Front Street
Traverse City   MI 49684
616 929-9201 or 616 264-9464

8   Bay West Antiques
221 Grand View Parkway
Traverse City   MI 49684
616 947-3211
Every day 10 to 6
Across from the power plant & Bay, 1/2 block west of Union.
25 dealers. Large variety.

9   Wilson Antiques
123 South Union Street
Traverse City   MI 49684
616 946-4177

10   The Firehouse Fair
118 Cass Street
Traverse City   MI 49684
616 935-4442   Gifts, housewares, reproductions, few antiques.

11   The Painted Door Gallery
154 East Front Street
Traverse City   MI 49684
616 929-4988

Map: Traverse City:

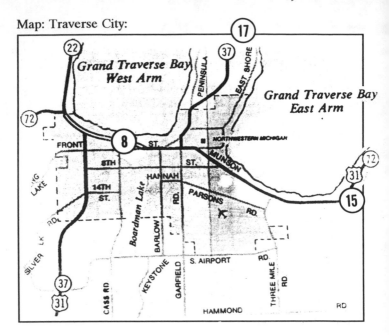

12   Fascinations
140 East Front Street
Traverse City MI 49684
616 922-0051
Second floor rear of the Arcade Mini-Mall.
Collectibles, some antiques.

13   Oberschulte Gallery
544 East Eighth Street
Traverse City   MI 49684
616 946-0424   Parking in back of the small shop.

14   Rickman's Antiques
628 Fern Street
Traverse City   MI 49684
616 946-6609

15   Antique Company - East Bay
4386 U.S. 31 North
Traverse City   MI 49684
616 938-3000
Daily: 10 to 6
Winter hours: Jan., Feb., March & April: Fri., Sat. & Sun.
10 to 6
East Bay, just south of Acme, beside the Traverse Bay
Woolen Company and Troutman.
General line of items circa 1880-1950.

16   Cherry Acres Antiques
12396 Peninsula Drive
Traverse City   MI 49484
616 223-4813
8 miles north on Peninsula Drive.

17   Walt's Antiques
2513 Nelson Rd
Traverse City   MI 49686
616 223-4123; or home 616 223-7386
E-mail: feiger@gtii.com
Web page: www.michigantravler.com/antiques
Spring, Summer & Fall: 7 days a week 10 to 6;
Winter: by chance or appointment.
Old Mission Peninsula, eight miles north of Traverse City on
M-37, west one half mile on Nelson Road to the barn.
Antique gas pumps, advertising, flow blue, vintage clothing,
and other rare and common antiques.

WILLIAMSBURG

18   Bunk House Antiques
9866 M-72
Williamsburg   MI 49690
616 267-5622

ACME

19   Hobart's
5698 North U.S. 31
Acme   MI 49610
616 938-1777

9.4 Kalkaska County

KALKASKA

1   Kalkaska Antiques
324 South Cedar Street (U.S. 131)
Kalkaska MI
616 258-550

© 1998 AAA - used by permission.

2   Somewhere in Time Antiques
552 West Fair Lake Road
Kalkaska MI 48744
616 258-5653

RAPID CITY

3   Millers Antiques
Downtown Rapid City
Rapid City   MI 49676
616 331-6104

4   Kayle & Agnes Doty, Marilyn Doty Larson Antiques
6898 Crystal Beach Road
Rapid City   MI 49676
616 322-2807
Summer: Daily 10 to 4; Sunday by chance.
North side of road, 1 mile west of County Road 597.
Clocks, country furniture, pewter, folkart, stoneware, copper
and brass, handwoven rugs, & general line.

MANCELONA

5 KG & Co.
7820 U.S. 131 N.E.
Mancelona MI 49659
616 258-1100; Fax: 616 258-6729
Oct. to May: Thurs. to Sun. 10 to 5:30, or by chance or
appointment;
June to Oct.: Open 6 days 10 to 5 (Thurs. to Tues.), closed
Wed. "Watch for the Flags."
Midway between Mancelona and Kalkaska, just south of Twin
Lake Road.
Antiques, collectibles, gift items, plus quality furniture
refinishing products & repairs.
Outside sales June, July, August.

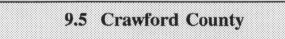

9.5 Crawford County

> Map on Following Page <

GRAYLING

1   Grayling Antique Mall
100 Michigan Street
Grayling MI 49738
517 348-2113
May be closing in early 1999.

2   Au Sable Antiques & Dulcimer Co.
235 M-72 West
Grayling MI 49738   517 348-5972

3 Annendale Antiques
576 Wesman Drive
Grayling   MI 49738
517 348-2130
Daily 9 to 5, closed Wed.; evenings by appointment.
8 miles west of Grayling on M-72 at Manistee River Bridge.
General line of antiques, lots of glass and children's dishes.

Map: Crawford & Oscoda Counties:

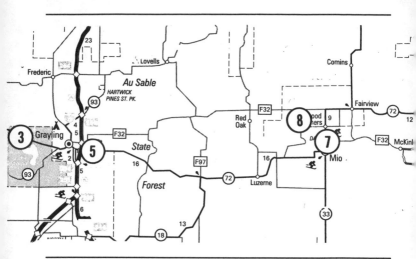

© 1998 AAA - used by permission.

4   Potbelly Antiques
4729 North Down River Road
Grayling MI 49738
517 348-8578

5   South Branch Antiques
7901 East M-72
Grayling   MI 49738
517 348-2514
May to Sept.: Thurs. to Mon. 9 to 5; rest of the year by
chance or appointment.
Two miles west of M-18, north side of the road.
General line of antiques.

9.6 Oscoda County

> Map st Top of This Page <

MIO

6   Aunty's Antiques
1743 South M-33
Mio MI 48647   517 826-6041

7   Granny's Antiques
109 East 8th Street
Mio   MI 48647
517 826-5674
April 15 to Dec. 1: Mon. to Sat. 11 to 5, Sun. 11 to 3;
Dec. 1 to April 15: Sat. 11 to 5, Sun. 11 to 3
North side of street, a half block east of downtown blinker light.
Lot's of Glassware, furniture, and other old general items.

8   The Stables
1665 West Kittle Road
Mio MI 48647
517 826-5454
Most of the time: Daily 10 to 5, Sun. 12 to 5
South side of the road, 3.3 miles west of M-33. Kittle Road is 3 miles north of Mio.
Glassware, quilts, general household, linens-furniture.

DRIVING DISTANCES IN THE LOWER PENINSULA:

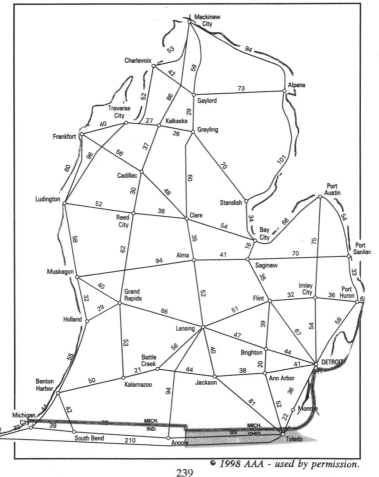

© *1998 AAA - used by permission.*

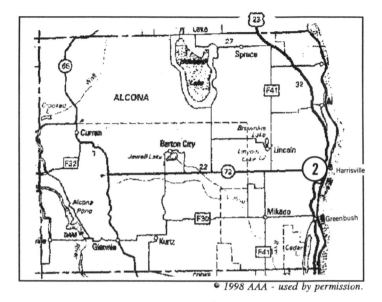

© 1998 AAA - used by permission.

GREENBUSH

1   The Cedar Closet
4034 U.S. 23 South
Greenbush MI 48738
517 739-2632 (home phone)

HARRISVILLE

2   Lake Street Daisy's
115 Lake Street
Harrisville MI 48740
517 724-6229
Summer: 7 days a week 11 to 5 (Memorial Day to Labor Day)
Winter: By chance (weekends through Christmas).
Off U.S. 23, north of Oscoda, across the street from Lake
Huron, next to Alcona Review.
Marble tables, furniture, Hull Pottery, and home-made fudge.

3   Kenneth Roy Antiques
312 South U.S. 23
Harrisville MI 48742
517 724-5600

TIER 10:
THE M-32 ROUTE

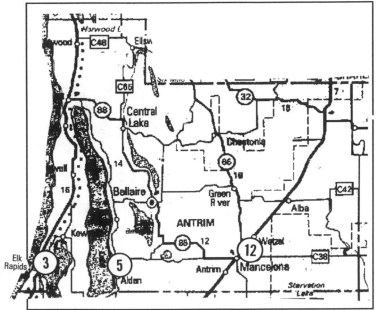

© 1998 AAA - used by permission.

KEWADIN

1   Sentimental Journey Antiques
7224 Cherry Avenue, east end of town
Kewadin MI 49648
616 264-6955

ELK RAPIDS

2 A Summer Place Ltd.
125 River Street
Elk Rapids   MI 49629
616 264-6556; (off season: 517 631-0509)

3   Harbor Antiques
151 River Street
Elk Rapids   MI 49629
616 264-6850
Mon. to Sat. 10 to 6, Sun. 10 to 4
Downtown, east side of the street.
Quality furniture, glassware, pottery, etc.
New mall opened 1998; 6,000 square feet, 50 plus dealer
capacity.

Harbor Antiques

151 River Street
Elk Rapids, MI 49629

(616) 264-6850

Open 7 Days -- Plus Evenings

Wednesday Street Festival in Summer

15 Minutes North of Traverse City

5 Miles North of the Grand Taverse Resort

25 Minutes South of Charlevoix

Garden & Farmers Market Courtyard

● *Limited Dealer Space Available* ●

ALDEN

4   Antrim Antiques
9053 Helena Street
Alden   MI 49612
616 331-6562   Quilts; hunting & fishing collectibles.

5   Talponia Books Ltd.
10545 Coy
Alden MI 49612
616 331-6324

6   Cottage Antiques
10366 E. Torch Lake Road
Alden MI 49615
616 331-6066

7   Jean Ann Antiques
9046 Helena Road
Alden   MI 49615
616 331-4261

BELLAIRE

8   Poor Mary's Cottage Antiques
408 North Bridge Street
Bellaire   MI 49615
616 377-7504

CENTRAL LAKE

9   Dorothy Mulonas Antiques
South Main Street (M-88)
Central Lake MI 49622   616 544-6734

TORCH LAKE VILLAGE

10   School House Antiques
2592 U.S. 31 North
Torch Lake Village MI 49627
616 599-2056

EASTPORT

11   D & J Antiques
6067 North M-88 (U.S. 31 & M-88)
Eastport   MI 49627
616 599-2710

MANCELONA

12   Dee's Antiques
301 South Maple, east of U.S. 131
Mancelona   MI 49659
616 587-8121

13   Red Windmill Antiques
3775 Docrr Road, at U.S. 131
Mancelona   MI 49659
616 587-5121

*Note:
a shop with a
Mancelona
address is
located in
Kalkaska
County,
Section 9.4.*

Map: Otsego & Montmorency Counties:

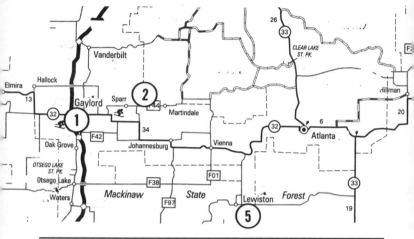

© 1998 AAA - used by permission.

GAYLORD

1   Antiques Out of the Blue
237 South Wisconsin Street
Gaylord MI 49735
517 731-6053
Mon. to Sat. 10:30 to 5:30, Sun. 1 to 4
West of downtown, south of Route 32 two blocks; next to
Dan's TV.
Flow Blue, antique clocks, handmade baskets, & general line
of antiques.

2   Duck Creek Antiques
1273 Duck Creek Trail
Gaylord MI 49735
517 732-3972
Fri. & Sat. 10 to 5, Sun. 12 to 4
From Gaylord take M-32 east to Wilkinson Road (F-44)
turning left. Wilkinson Road to Marquardt Road (F-44) to
Sparr Road. Turn right on Sparr Road (F-44). From Sparr
Mall continue east 2.3 miles to private "Duck Creek Trail" and
turn left (north) only. If the flag is out they are open. About
eight miles east of Gaylord.
Country collectibles, primitives, folk art.

3   The Castle
403 South Otsego
Gaylord MI 49785
517 732-4665

JOHANNESBURG

4   Cozy Corners Antiques
10816 M-32 East
Johannesburg MI 49751   517 732-2225

10.3 Montmorency County

> Map on Preceding Page <

LEWISTON

5   Antiques Depot Mall
5030 County Road 612
Lewiston MI 49756
517 786-4897
May to Dec.: Daily 10 to 4:30;
Jan. to April: Fri. & Sat. 10:30 to 4:30
Corner of County Roads 489 & 612.
seven blocks east of town center.
Cut glass & general line.

10.4 Alpena County

> Map on Following Page <

ALPENA

1   Country Cupboard
102 North Second
Alpena MI 49707
517 356-6020
Mon. to Fri. 10 to 5:30, Sat. 10 to 5, Sun. 12 to 4
Downtown
Unique old drug store; antiques, collectibles, country gifts.

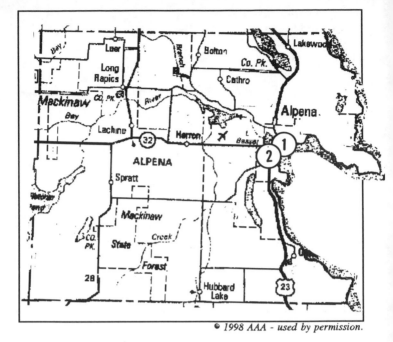

© 1998 AAA - used by permission.

2   Helen's Antiques & Gifts
127 North 2nd Avenue
Alpena MI 49707
517 356-3298
Mon. to Sat. 10 to 5:30
East end of downtown, northwest corner River Street & 2nd
Avenue. Glassware, jewelry, furniture, collectibles, gifts, and
Beanie Babies.

3   Artis Antique Mall & Artis Books & Antiques
201 & 209 North Second
Alpena MI 49707
517 354-3401

4   Kathy's Bargain Barn
6465 U.S. 23 North, five miles north
Alpena MI 49707
517 354-3070

HUBBARD LAKE

5   C. Leigh's
13822 Hubbard Lake Road
Hubbard Lake MI 49747
517 727-2362

TIER 11:
SOUTH OF MACKINAC

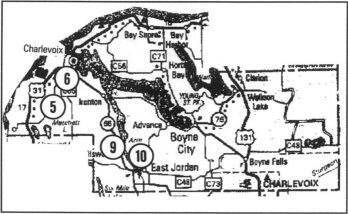

© 1998 AAA - used by permission.

CHARLEVOIX

1   The Sisters Antiques
U.S. 31 South
Charlevoix   MI 49720
616 547-6457; 616 547-6914

2   The Garage Sale
755 Petoskey Ave. (U.S. 31 North)
Charlevoix   MI 49720
616 547-5700

3   North Seas Gallery
330 Bridge Street
Charlevoix   MI 49720
616 547-0422; 616 547-2959

4   Rose Cottage Antiques
107 Mason Street, west of Bridge Street
Charlevoix   MI 49720
616 547-0636, or 616 547-5842

5   Kelly Antiques & Restoration

Antiques: 06176 Old U.S. 31 South
Restoration: 10696 Ferry Road
Charlevoix MI 49720
Antiques: 616 547-9409
Restoration: 616 547-6755; E-mail: fmwilson@freeway.net
Open Year round by chance or appointment; open most
evenings & weekends.
Antiques: One and a half miles south of Charlevoix go left on
Old U.S. 31 after Brumm's Studio Showroom; .6 mile on the
left.
Restoration: 5.5 miles south on M-66 to Ironton, then right
onto Ferry Road; one quarter mile on the left.
The antique division specializes in wood & wicker furniture
(and wicker repair).
The restoration division specializes in antique furniture
restoration.

6   Wishes & Whimsies Gifts and Antiques

1208 Bridge Street
Charlevoix   MI 49720
616 547-6766
Summer: Daily 10 to 5; Nov. to April: closed Mon. & Tues.
South of downtown on U.S. 31.
General line of antiques; also porcelain, pottery & glass
repair.

7   Shop of All Crafters
704 Bridge Street
Charlevoix   MI 49720
616 547-0257
Mission oak.

8   Proposed Mall
Bridge Street
Charlevoix   MI 49720
New mall proposed to open in 1999, but address and details
not made available.

■■■   EAST JORDAN   ■■■

9   Stonehedge Antiques

02195 M-66 North
East Jordan   MI 49720
616 547-5527
Memorial Day to Mid-Oct.: Wed. to Sat. 10 to 5, Sun. 12 to 4;
July & Aug.: 7 days a week.
West side of highway, 1.25 miles south of Ironton Ferry.

10   Busy Bridge Antiques & Gifts

207 Main Street
East Jordan   MI 49727
616 536-3511
Open all year: Mon. to Sat. 10 to 5:30;
Sun. in July to Dec.: 11 to 4
Downtown.   Note: there is no sign pointing the way to
downtown from M-66; go east at the light and cross the
bridge and go left at Main Street.
General line of antiques; also antiques in the basement and
second floor.

Map: City of Charlevoix:

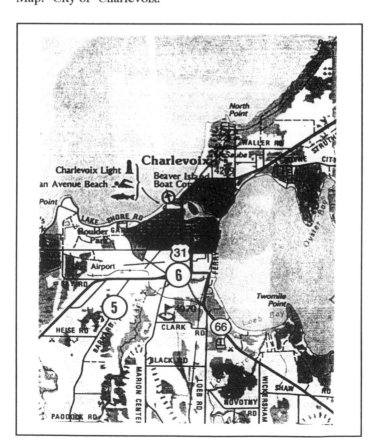

11.2 Emmet County

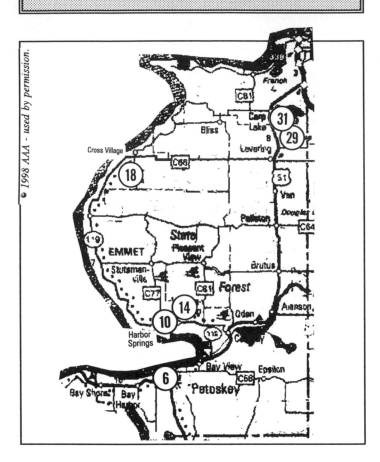

© 1998 AAA - used by permission.

PETOSKEY

1   Amish Way Antiques
08600 Camp Daggett Road
Petoskey   MI 49770
616 347-3898

2   Joseph's World Classic Antiques
2680 Charlevoix Avenue (U.S. 31 South)
Petoskey MI 49770
616 347-0121
19th & 20th Century decorative arts; a few antiques.

3   Marietta Antique Shop
106 East Mitchell Street (U.S. 31)
Petoskey   MI 49770
616 347-8369

250

4   J C's Antiques
203-A Howard Street
Petoskey   MI 49770
616 348-0840

5   Longton Hall Antiques
410 Rose Street
Petoskey   MI 49770
616 347-9672

6   Jedediahs Antiques
422 E. Mitchell Street
Petoskey   MI 49770
616 347-1919
Mon. to Sat. 10 to 5
Downtown, across from Pennsylvania Park.
Featuring dealers from Canada to California carrying a
multitude of regional pieces.

7   Joie De Vie Antiques
1901 M-119 (Harbor-Petoskey Road)
Petoskey   MI 49770
616 347-1400

Petoskey Antiques Festival
Emmet County Fairgrounds, U.S. 31 South; Sat. 10 to 5, Sun.
10 to 4   July 3 & 4 and July 31-Aug. 1, 1999

■■■ HARBOR SPRINGS ■■■

8   Grant Interiors
8442 Harbor Petoskey Road (M-119 North), in Harbor Plaza
Harbor Springs MI 49770
616 347-8824   Home furnishings & design; a few antiques.

9   Joie de Vie Antiques
138 East Main Street
Harbor Springs   MI 49740
616 526-7700

10   Huzza
136 Main Street East
Harbor Springs   MI 49740
616 526-2128
Summer: Mon. to Sat. 9:30 to 6;
Winter 10 to 5; closed Mar. & April
Downtown, south side of street.
Antiques, interior design, home accessories.

11   Patricia Woods Antiques
120 East Main
Harbor Springs   MI 49740
616 526-9691

12   L'Esprit
195 West Main & 220 State Street
Harbor Springs   MI 49740
616 526-9888
E-mail: lesprit@lesprit.com   Web site: www.lesprit.com;

13   Elliott & Elliott
292 East Third Street
Harbor Springs MI 49740
616 526-2040

14   Bishop's Antiques & Fine Arts Gallery
378 Third Street, at Judd Street
Harbor Springs   MI 49740
616 526-8075

15   Pooter Olooms
39 State Street
Harbor Springs   MI 49740
616 526-6101
Scandinavian country pine, quilts, folk art. 3,200 sq. ft.

GOOD HART

16   TLC Summer Place
811 North Lakeshore (M-119)
Good Hart MI 49723
616 526-7538

17   Good Hart Antiques
M-119
Good Hart   MI 49737
616 526-9533

CROSS VILLAGE

18   Rose's Antiques & Collectibles
5550 North Lakeshore Drive (M-119)
Cross Village MI 49723
616 526-5934
April to Dec.: Usually every day 10 to 5:30.
1.5 miles south of Cross Village.
Everything from farm tools to furniture.

19   The Red House at Cross Village
M-119 & State Road
Cross Village   MI 49723
616 526-2343

CONWAY

20   Desiree's Country Nostalgia
2343 Cook Avenue (West Conway Road)
Conway   MI 49722
616 347-8661

21   Oden Antiques
Highway 31
Oden   MI 49764

ALANSON

22   Second Hand Man & Crooked River Rustic
7493 U.S. 31
Alanson   MI 49706
616 548-5173

23   Regina's Lakeview Antiques
M-68 West
Alanson   MI 49706
616 548-5398

BRUTUS

24   Adams Antiques
3771 U.S. 31
Brutus   MI 49716
616 529-6596

25   Graham's Antiques
1812 Gregory Road
Brutus   MI 49716
616 539-8275

PELLSTON

26   Town & Country Antiques
128 Stenson (U.S. 31)
Pellston   MI 49769
616 539-8340
Small shop; used items & some antiques.

27   Antiques, Art & Collectibles
114 North Stimpson (U.S. 31)
Pellston MI 49769
616 539-8030

28   Blue Barn Antiques & Collectibles
123 Stimpson (U.S. 31)
Pellston MI 49769
616 539-8550; 616 439-0940

LEVERING

29   Gaslight Antiques & Collectibles
7116 N. U.S. 31
Levering MI 49755
616 537-4446
Mid May to Mid Oct.: Mon. to Sat. 11 to 5:30; Closed Thur.,
Sun. by chance only
2 miles North of Levering blinker light, east side of highway.
General line Antiques and Collectibles, wicker, lamps, pottery,
primitives, 50's, etc.

30   Levering Antiques & Rustic Furniture
1 Robinson Street
Levering MI 49755
616 537-4972

31   Little Bit Country
7010 U.S. 31
Levering MI 49755
616 537-2525
May 1 through Oct.: Daily 9 to 5:30;
Nov. & Dec.: weekends or by chance.
Between Levering and Carp Lake.
Antiques, collectibles, hand-made crafts and country items.
Shop was for sale at the time of the survey; may close in 1999.

CARP LAKE

32   Old Tyme Treasures
6478 Gill Road, at U.S. 31
Carp Lake   MI 49718
616 537-2229

33   The Maples Resort & Antiques
8982 Paradise Trail (Old U.S. 31)
Carp Lake   MI 49718
616 537-4814   Glassware, bronze, & general line.

© 1998 AAA - used by permission.

INDIAN RIVER

1 Bearly Used Antiques & Treasures
6033 East M-68
Indian River MI 49749
Residence: 616 238-9772
May 15 thru October 15: daily 10 to 5
South side of highway, just west of I-75 Exit 310.
Specialize in glassware and china.

2 Of Cabbages & Kings Gift Shop
Downtown Indian River
MI 49749 M-27
616 238-7700   Gifts, a few antiques.

CHEBOYGAN

3   Treasure Hunt Flea Market & Antiques
405 Duncan Avenue
Cheboygan MI 49721   616 627-6080

11.4 Presque Isle County

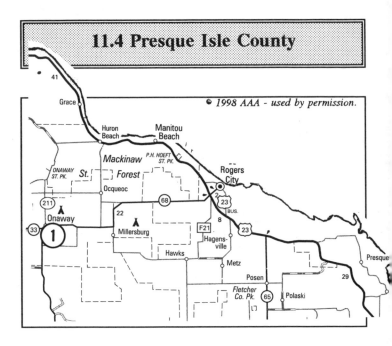

● *1998 AAA - used by permission.*

ONAWAY

1   Everlasting Things Antique Mall and Bargain Barn
20775 Washington
Onaway   MI 49765
517 733-6532
Memorial Day Weekend through Nov.: Wed. to Sat. 10 to 5;
Dec. to Memorial Day Weekend by chance or appointment.
Adjacent to historic courthouse.

2   And Yesterday's Trash
Highway M-33, Hackett Lake Highway
Onaway   MI 49765
517 733-6434   Primitives, old logging tools, etc.

3   Antiques & More
20451 State Street
Onaway   MI 49765
517 733-4449

TIER 12:
THE UPPER
PENINSULA

12.01 Mackinac County

Map: Mackinac, Chippewa & Luce Counties:

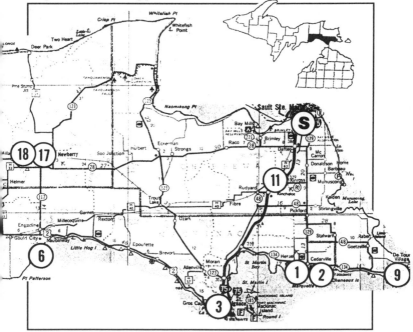

S = Sault Ste. Marie: 12 - 14

--- **HESSEL** ---

1   Hessel Marketplace
Highway M-134
Hessel MI 49745
906 484-3002
Summer: Mon. to Sat. 10 to 5;
Fall & Winter: By chance or appointment - Jeri Griffin
906 484-3762
At the light in Hessel.
General line of antiques and collectibles in shop and barn;
also gifts, handmade baskets, workshops.

CEDARVILLE

2   I Remember When
Highway 134
Cedarville MI 49719
906 484-2495
May through July: Daily 10 to 5;
Aug. Mon. to Sat. 10 to 5;
Sept. through Nov. Mon. & Thurs. through Sat. 10 to 5
Half mile south of downtown, next to Autore Oil Co., west side of highway.
Antiques, gifts, birdhouses.

ST. IGNACE

3   The Emporium
110 North State Street
St. Ignace MI 49781
906 643-6565; fax: 906-643-0113
E-mail: KPbrady@up.net; Web page: www.ignace.com
Open year round, Mon. to Sat. 9 to 5. Open Sun. by appointment.
Downtown across from Arnold Ferry.
Specializing in Antique lighting and furniture.

4   Treasures & Trinkets (& The Unique Shop)
334 North State Street
St. Ignace MI 49781
906 643-6622
Gifts, Indian Jewelry, figurines, pewter, glassware.

5   Anchor In Antiques
2122 West U.S. Highway 2, eight miles west
St. Ignace MI 49781
906 643-8112
Great Lakes Nautical Items & general line of antiques.

NAUBINWAY

6   Uncle Tom's Antiques
Blake & Main Streets
Naubinway MI 49762
906 477-6259
June, July, Aug. 10 to 5
From U.S. Highway 2: south at the blinker light one block, then east two blocks. Follow the signs.
General line, plus fishing & hunting and rustic & primitive collectibles.

GOULD CITY

7   Northwoods Antiques
West Milakokia Lake Road, 2 miles south of U.S. 2
Gould City MI 49838
906 477-6991

12.02 Chippewa County

> Map in Previous Section. <

DE TOUR VILLAGE

8   Log Cabin Antiques & Collectibles
637 Ontario Street, across from the marina
De Tour Village MI 49725
906 297-2502

9   Red Oaks Antiques and Collectibles
16185 East M-134 #68B
De Tour Village MI 49725
906 297-2404
May 1 to Oct: Every day 10 to 5
7 miles west of town.

PICKFORD

10   Items Out of the Past
Main Street (MI Highway 129)
Pickford MI
906 647-9942   Located in Pickford Floral & Gifts.

KINCHELOE

11   Building 313
5189 West M-80 Suite G
Kincheloe/Kinross   MI 49788
906 495-5378
Mon. to Fri. 11 to 5, Sat. 10 to 3; Jan.-April: Wed. by appt.
I-75 Exit 378; Town & Country Plaza Carpet, Antiques &
Flea Market Mall.
Several theme rooms, including: sewing, dolls & toys, kitchen
& glassware, furniture; also gifts, an herb shop, and a
Christmas Shop.

SAULT STE. MARIE

12   La Galerie
1420 Ashmun Street
Sault Ste. Marie MI 49783
906 635-1044
All year: Mon. to Sat. 10 to 5; Sun. 12 to 4
Corner of 6th Avenue on I-75 Business Spur.
General antiques and collectibles.

13   Silver Lining Antiques
530 Ashmun Street
Sault Ste. Marie MI 49783
906 632-4929
Tues. to Sat. 10 to 6, or by appointment.
Heart of downtown, 3 doors down from the Soo Theater.
Antique furniture, jewelry, pottery, cookware, linens, china,
silver, crystal.

14   Austin Oak & Tobacco Shop
539 Ashmun Street
Sault Ste. Marie MI 49783
906 635-1242
Mon. to Thurs. 9 to 5:30, Fri. 9 to 7, Sat. 9 to 5
Downtown, across from Soo Theater.
Basement full of antiques; also Amish furniture.

BRIMLEY

15   Willow Grove Farms
Highway M-28, 4 miles west of I-75
Brimley MI 49715
906 248-5168   Antiques, herbs, flowers.

12.03 Luce County

> **Map in Previous Section <**

NEWBERRY

16   Falls Hotel Antiques
301 Newberry Ave. (MI Highway 123)
Newberry MI 49868   In lobby of historic hotel & restaurant.

17 Antiques By Donelle
101 East John Street
Newberry MI 49868
906 293-8044; res.: 906 586-9544
Tues. to Fri. 10 to 5, or by chance; closed March.
Half block east of Highway 123, north side of street.
Fine glass and vintage clothing.

18 Country Gallery
607 Newberry Avenue (MI Route 123)
Newberry   MI 49868
906 293-8262
June to Oct.: Mon to Sat. 9;30 a.m. to 9 p.m.; Sun. 11 TO 6;
Winter: Mon. to Sat. 9:30 to 5:30
South of downtown, east side of street, across from the school.
Mostly gifts, some antiques.
Also: Antique 1940's soda fountain.
(For contemporary rustic furniture visit the U.P. Trading Co.)

19   Pine Ridge Antique Mall
207 Handy Street
Newberry   MI 49868
No telephone listed.

20   Katie's Antiques
Rt.4 Box 1095
Newberry MI 49868
906 293-5766
East on Route 28 to Route 117, left 1 mile to Red Camp Rd.

━━━━━━━━━━   **McMILLAN**   ━━━━━━━━━━

21   Farmhouse Antiques
County Road 438
McMillan MI 49853
906 293-8792

Schoolcraft, Alger & Delta Counties:

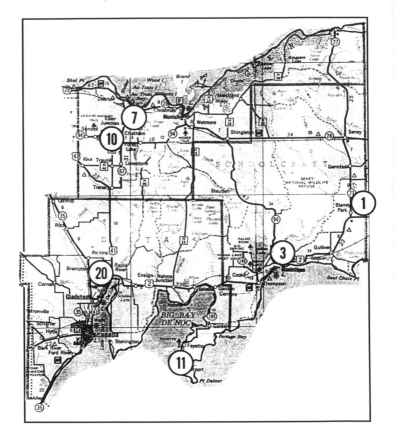

GERMFASK

1   Suzantiques
Highway 77 - Blaney Park
Route 1 Box 59-A
Germfask MI 49836
906 586-3135
Year round, random hours.
Two miles north of Highway 2, seven miles south of
Germfask, east side of highway.
General line of antiques; postcards and other paper
ephemera.

BLANEY PARK

2   Paul Bunyan's Country Store
Michigan Highway 77, north of U.S. 2
Blaney Park   MI 49836
906 283-3861
Antiques, plus a real general store.

MANISTIQUE

3   Christophers
211 Oak Street
Manistique MI 49854
906 341-2570
April 1 to Jan. 1: Every day 9 to 8;
Winter: Mon. to Sat. 9 to 5
Downtown, just east of the post office.
Two floors of a general line of antiques.

4   Maple Cottage
227 Maple St.
Manistique MI 49854
No telephone.

5   Manistique Floral Phantasmagoria
233 Walnut Street
Manistique MI 49854
888 844-6620
Antiques, art & flowers.

6   Hampton's Antiques
1152 West Lakeshore Dr.
Manistique MI 49854
906 341-5350

DRIVING
DISTANCES
IN THE UPPER PENINSULA

12.05 Alger County

> Map in Previous Section <

AUTRAIN

7   Red Barn Antiques at LaValley's Resort
N-7017 AuTrain-Lake Road Highway 3
Au Train MI 49806
906 892-8455
Mon. to Thurs. 10 to 6, or by appointment.
Two miles south of M-28.
General line, specializing in 1940's to 1960's furniture &
decorative objects.

MUNISING

8   Old Northlight Antiques & Gifts
M-28 East
Munising MI 49862
906 387-2109

9   The Bay House
111 Elm Avenue
Munising MI 49862
906 387-4253

EBEN JUNCTION

10   One of a Kind Antiques & Collectibles
E2814 M-94
Eben Junction MI 49825
906 439-5764
E-mail: sswaim@chatham.tds.net
Tues. to Sat. 10 to 5, or by appointment.
North side of highway, west of Eben Junction

12.06 Delta County

> Map in Previous Section <

FAYETTE

11   Fayette Antiques
2251 II Road (County Road 183)
MAIL: Garden
Fayette MI 49835
906 644-2620; 906 644-2401
June 1 to Sept. 15: Tues. to Sun. 10 to 6
Seven miles south of Fayette State Park.
Antiques & unique things; garden items, primitives, fine dishes.

GLADSTONE

12   Chicken Coop Antiques
7051 P Road
Gladstone MI 49837
906 786-1150

13   Fort Wells Antiques
(Bay View Furniture Stripping & Antiques)
7097 P Road
Gladstone MI 49837
906 786-4264

14   Foxx Den Antiques
7509 U.S. 2 & 41 & M-35
Gladstone   MI 49837
906 786-9014

15   Backstage Antiques
7272 U.S. 2 & 41 & M-35
Gladstone   MI 49837
906 789-7050

KIPLING

16   Keepsake Workshop & Antiques
8905 23.15 Street
Kipling MI 49837
906 428-4275
Old Highway 2 between Gladstone & Rapid River.

ESCANABA

17   The Market Place
1011 Ludington Street
Escanaba MI 49829
906 789-1326
Co-op shop; opened 1985; 25 dealers.   Antiques & crafts.

18   The Belle Pearl
121 S. 11th Street
Escanaba MI 49829
906 789-0041; 906 786-4919
Located in old City Hall building, a half block south of
Ludington Street.   Note: there is no significant sign indicating
there are any shops in the building.

19   Reminisce Antique Mall
1215 Ludington Street
Escanaba MI 49829
906 786-0772

RAPID RIVER

20   U.P. Treasure Hunters Antique Mall
7946 U.S. Route 2
Rapid River MI 49878
906 474-5049
E-mail: kencharlebois@uplogon.com
Web page: www.class.idsite.com
Ebay Auction Code Name: YOOPER
By Chance: May & Nov.; June to Oct. anytime by chance 10
to 6
U.S. 2 & Rapid River, north side of the highway.
Rocks & minerals; general line of antiques; unique furniture
& carvings.

21   Little Bit of Everything
7885 U.S. Highway 2
Rapid River MI 49878
906 474-6774
Next to Dairy Flo, south side of highway.

22   Northern Exposure Flea Market
Highway 2 East
Rapid River MI 49878
906 474-9998
Building was for sale at time of survey.

12.07 Menominee County

> Map on the Following Page <

MENOMINEE

1   Colonial Corner Antiques
1728 7th Street
Menominee MI 49858
906 863-5221

12.08 Dickinson County

> Map on the Following Page <

IRON MOUNTAIN

2   Cobweb Antiques
N-3956 North U.S. Highway 2
Iron Mountain MI 49801
906 774-6560
Mon. to Sat. 1 to 4
Just south of the M-95 & U.S. 2 junction.
Furniture and general line of antiques.

3   Edie's Interiors & Antique Mall
531 South Stevenson (U.S. 2)
Iron Mountain MI 49801
906 774-1851
Mon. to Sat. 9 to 5;
Thanksgiving to Christmas also open Sun. 12 to 4
Downtown, at B Street.
General line of antiques.
Parking in the rear.

NORWAY

4   Norway Antique Mall
729 Main Street
Norway MI 49870
906 563-8246

Menominee, Dickinson & Marquette Counties:

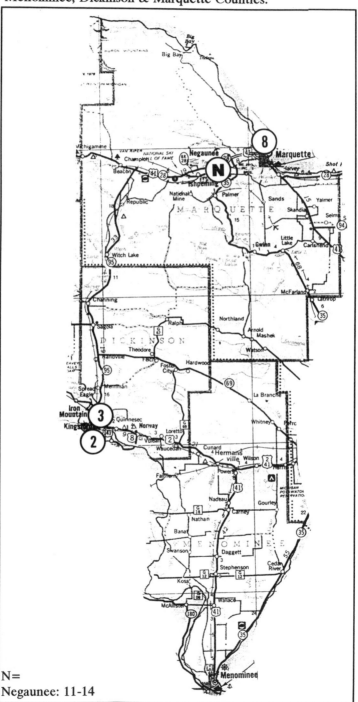

N=
Negaunee: 11-14

HARVEY

5   Antique Village
2296 U.S. 41 South
Harvey   MI 49855
906 249-3040

Map: City of Marquette:

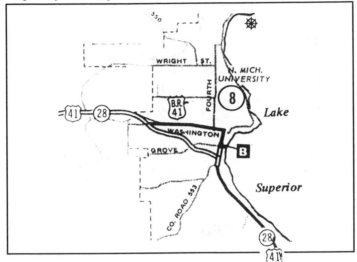

MARQUETTE

6   The Collector Antiques
214 South Front
Marquette MI 49855
906 228-4134

7   Fagan's Antiques
333 West Washington
Marquette MI 49855
906 228-4311

8   Summer Cottage
810 North Third Street
Marquette MI 49855
906 226-2795
Summer: Mon. to Sat. 10 to 5, Sun. 12 to 4;
Winter: Mon. to Sat. 11 to 5
North of downtown, east side of the street.
Ten decorated rooms in a quaint historic home surrounded by
a cottage garden. Decorative antiques and fine gifts.
(Say hello to Sawyer the white cat.)

9   Past and Presents
116 West Spring Street, half block west of U.S. 41
Marquette   MI 49885
906 226-8533

10   Peddler's Hill
325 Erickson Avenue, behind Bonanza
Marquette MI 49855
906 225-0155

NEGAUNEE

11   Old Bank Building Antiques
331 Iron Street
Negaunee MI 49866
906 475-4777
Mon. to Sat. 10 to 5, Sun. 12 to 4
Downtown
General line of antiques; large three-story shop.

12   Kate's Collectibles
28 U.S. 41 East
Negaunee MI 49866
906 475-4443
Mon. to Sat. 10 to 5, Sun. 12 to 5
South side of highway, one mile east of town.
Fine general line of antiques.

13   Midtown Architectural Antiques & Bake Shoppe
317 Iron Street
Negaunee MI 49866
906 475-0064 or 906 475-5664 after hours
Open year-round: Mon. to Fri. 8 to 5, Sat. 10 to 5; plus
Sundays in summer.
Downtown
Architectural items, folk art, pottery, primitives, rustic items,
art glass, and gourmet desserts too.

14   Upper Level Design & Antiquities
415 Iron Street, Above Teddy's Florist
Negaunee MI 49866
906 475-4464

ISHPEMING

15   Paul's Jewelry & Gifts
209 South Main Street
Ishpeming MI 49849   Some antiques.

16   Just Browsing
206 Cleveland Avenue
Ishpeming MI 29849   906 485-6449

MICHIGAMME

17   Olde Millstream Antiques
Mill & Main Streets
Michigamme MI 49861   906 323-0023

18   The Red Door
U.S. Highway 41, three miles east
Michigamme MI 49861
906 323-6143   Antiques, gifts, gallery.

12.10 Iron County

> Map on the Following Page <

CRYSTAL FALLS

1   Bargain Barn Antiques
1340 West U.S. 2
Crystal Falls MI 49920
906 875-3381

2   Oldies But Goodies
801 Crystal Ave. (U.S. Highway 2 West)
Crystal Falls MI 49920
906 875-6294

3   Old Tradition Shop
612 Michigan Avenue
Crystal Falls MI 49920
906 875-4214

4   Junktion Antiques & Collectibles
1339 South U.S. 2
Crystal Falls MI 49920
906 875-4699
Mid-May to Mid-Nov.: Sun. to Fri. 12 to 6, Sat. 10 to 6,
closed Tues.
General line: glass, quilts, furniture, tools, etc.

Iron, Baraga, Houghton & Keweenaw Counties:

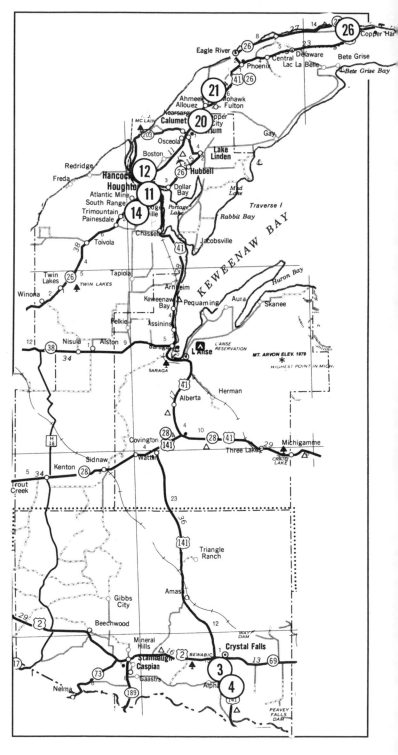

IRON RIVER

5   Ethel Joyce Turbessi at the Antique Cottage
545 West Ice Lake Road
Iron River MI 49935
906 265-9753 or 906 265-2756

6   Dobson's Antiques
4295 U.S. 2
Iron River MI 49935

12.11 Baraga County

> Map in Previous Section <

BARAGA

7   The Country Shop
Jurmu Road,Rte. 1 Box 66;
5 miles north off U.S. 41
Baraga MI 49908
906 353-7230

12.12 Houghton County

> Map in Previous Section <

CHASSELL

8   Eagle Shop
148 N. Wilson Drive (U.S. 41)
Chassell MI 49916
906 523-4423

9   Grandma's Antiques
300 Wilson Memorial Drive (U.S. 41)
Chassell MI 49916

10   Porch Antiques
447 U.S. 41
Chassell MI 49916
906 523-4819

HOUGHTON

11   Antique Mall
418 Sheldon Avenue
Houghton MI 49931
906 487-9483
Mon. to Sat. 10 to 5
Downtown, north side of the street.
General line, furniture & glass.

HANCOCK

12   Northwoods Trading Post
120 Quincy
Hancock MI 49930
906 482-5210

13   Quality Antique Furniture
807 U.S. Highway 41 North
Hancock MI 49930
906 482-4270
Inquire at Phil's Upholstery a block north.

SOUTH RANGE

14   Etc. Etc.
42 Tri Mountain Road (M-26)
South Range MI 49963
906 482-9171
Varied array of miscellaneous arts, crafts, and antiques.

LAURIUM

15   The Yard Sale
Helca & Third Streets
Laurium MI 49913

CALUMET

16   Copper World
101 Fifth Street
Calumet MI 49913
906 337-4016   New and old copper items.

17   The Garage Sale Store
6th & Oak Streets
Calumet MI 49913
906 337-0804

18   The Rose & The Thorn
451 Pine Street
Calumet MI 49913
906 337-1717
Ceramics & gifts 1st floor, antiques in basement.

19   J. Thiel & Associates
436 6th Street
Calumet MI 49913
906 337-1780

20   Antiquities
1156 Calumet Avenue (Highway 41)
Calumet MI 49913
906 337-5573
June through Aug.: Daily 12 to 8;
Sept. to Christmas: Fri. 4 to 8, Sat. 9 to 8, Sun. 12 to 8; April
& May: Fri. 4 to 8, Sat. 9 to 8, Sun. 12 to 8;
Red house across from the Calumet Information Center, at
the light.
Nicely displayed furniture, glassware, pottery, silver, etc.

12.13 Keweenaw County

> Map in Previous Section <

AHMEEK

21   True North Gallery
P.O. Box 141
Ahmeek MI 49901
906 337-1961
May through Oct: Tues. to Sun. 10 to 6;
Nov. through April: Fri. Sat. & Sun. 10 to 6
One block off U.S. 41.
Quality antique furniture, etc.

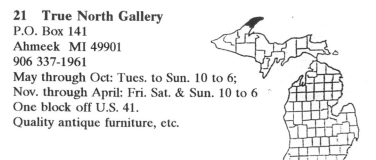

ALLOUEZ

22   The Last Place on Earth
U.S. 41   Box 76
Allouez MI 49805
906 337-1014

EAGLE RIVER

23   Leapfrog Collectibles
HCI Box 644
Eagle River MI 49950
906 337-6712
Highway 26 Downtown, in the old general store building.

EAGLE HARBOR

24   North Wind Books
HC 1 Box 190 Marina Road
Eagle Harbor MI 49950
906 289-4911
Marina Road east end of harbor, 1/2 mile from M-26.

25   Chit Chat Antiques & Collectibles
24 Sand Dunes Drive
Eagle Harbor MI 49950
906 289-4913

COPPER HARBOR

26   Minnetonka's Astor House Museum
U.S. 41 & MI Route 26
Copper Harbor MI 49918
906 289-4449
May 15 to Oct. 15: Every day 9 to 6
Center of town.
Antique shop & museum in back of the motel, antique fishing tackle, Indian relics, old books, bottles, mining memorabilia, etc.

27   Johnson's
U.S. 41 & MI 26
Copper Harbor MI 49918
North end of downtown.

28   Harbor Shop
745 MI Highway 26
Copper Harbor MI 49918

Gogebic & Ontonagon Counties:

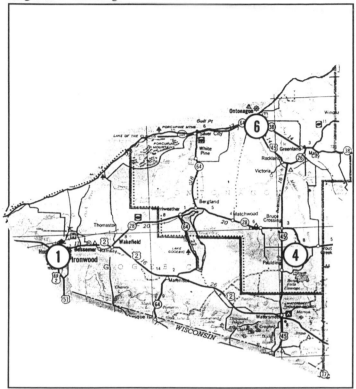

IRONWOOD

1   The Depot Antiques
318 Lake Street
Ironwood MI 49938
906 932-0900
Summer: Mon. to Sat. 9 to 5, Sun. 11 to 4;
Winter: Mon. to Sat. 10 to 4
East side of Ironwood, a block south of U.S. 2.

2   Doreen's Antiques
313 Lake Street
Ironwood MI 49938   906 932-4310

3   The Carriage House Antiques
303 South Lowell
Ironwood MI 49938
906 932-0766

12.15 Ontonagon County

> Map in Previous Section <

━━━━━━ BRUCE CROSSING ━━━━━━

4   Northern Lights Antiques & Artisans
575 Himanka Hill Road
Bruce Crossing MI 49912
906 827-3933
May 15 to Sept. 15: Every Day 11 to 5; Winter by chance.
South on U.S. 45 4 miles from Mich. Route 28, then east .9
mile. North side of road in brown metal building.
American Art Pottery; broad range of stock: over 10,000 items.

━━━━━━ ONTONAGON ━━━━━━

5   Victoria's Antiques
525 River Street
Ontonagon MI 49953   906 884-4400

6   Heritage Antique Mall
233 River Street
Ontonagon MI 49953   906 884-4747

INDEX OF DEALER SPECIALTIES

Index of Dealer Specialties - continued

Index of Dealer Specialties - continued